欢迎:中学汉语课本

HUANYING

An Invitation to Chinese Workbook

JIAYING HOWARD AND LANTING XU

VOLUME 3

3 / 1

PART 1

Cheng & Tsui Company

Boston

Published by
Cheng & Tsui Company, Inc.
25 West Street
Boston, MA 02111-1213 USA
Fax (617) 426-3669
www.cheng-tsui.com
"Bringing Asia to the World"™

ISBN 978-0-88727-741-2

Illustrations © by Murry R. Thomas, Landong Xu, Qiguang Xu, Lanting Xu, and Augustine Liu

Workbook design by Linda Robertson

CONTENTS

ONLINE RESOURCES

Audio Downloads

Throughout this workbook, you will see an audio CD icon to the left of many exercises. Audio CD icons indicate the presence of audio recordings, which are available as downloadable audio files. For information on how to download the audio files for this workbook, please see page iv of your *Huanying Volume 3* textbook.

TITLES OF RELATED INTEREST

The Way of Chinese Characters, 2nd Edition
The Origins of 670 Essential Words
By Jianhsin Wu, Illustrated by Chen Zheng, Chen Tian
Learn characters through a holistic approach.

Tales and Traditions, 2nd Edition *Volume 1: Fables, Myths, and Historical Figures*
Compiled by Yun Xiao, et al.
Read level-appropriate excerpts and adaptations from the Chinese folk and literary canon.

Cheng & Tsui Chinese Measure Word Dictionary
A Chinese-English / English-Chinese Usage Guide
Compiled by Jiqing Fang, Michael Connelly
Speak and write polished Chinese using this must-have reference.

Visit **www.cheng-tsui.com** to view samples, place orders, and browse other language-learning materials.

第一单元　新学期

UNIT 1　A New Semester

1.1　新同学
A New Student

一 · 听力练习

**I. Match Them!**

Listen to Audio Clip 1-1-1. Match the phrases you hear with the characters in Column B. Enter the corresponding numbers in Column A.

Column A 你听到的	Column B 汉字
	新来的
	没见过
	开玩笑
	做研究
	希望你去
	借读一年
	进步很快
	甜言蜜语
	特别理解
	互相学习
	大学教授

	转学来这儿
	把家搬到
	多么幸运啊
	将来回美国
	在美国出生
	一直住在法国

II. Listen to the recording of Dialogue 1 from Lesson 1.1 first, and then answer the True/False questions in Audio Clip 1-1-2.

	1	2	3	4
对				
错				

III. Listen to the recording of Dialogue 2 from Lesson 1.1 first, and then answer the True/False questions in Audio Clip 1-1-3.

	1	2	3	4
对				
错				

IV. Answer the questions in this section based on your understanding of the Lesson 1.1 dialogues.

Directions: Listen carefully to the questions in Audio Clip 1-1-4 and record your answers on an audio recorder. If you do not have a recording device, you can write down your answers below in pinyin or characters.

1. _____

2. _____

3. _____

   _____

4. _____

   _____

   _____

5. _____

   _____

   _____

   _____

   _____

6. _____

7. _____

8. _____

   _____

   _____

   _____

V. It is the first day of a new semester. You are helping your friend Linda move into the dorm. Listen carefully to Linda's instructions in Audio Clip 1-1-5 and place each item where she says it should go.

Items to be placed in the room:

VI. You posted a new photo of yourself and your friends on a social networking site. Your Chinese friend saw it and wants to ask you a few questions about the people in the photo. Listen carefully to the questions in Audio Clip 1-1-6 and answer them with as much detail as you can. Try to speak for at least 20 seconds when answering each question. You can take notes in the space provided below.

Notes:

_____

_____

_____

_____

_____

_____

二·综合语言练习

I. How do you say it in Chinese?

1. I transferred here this semester.

_____

2. It is fortunate that my Chinese has progressed rapidly.

_____

3. I was born in San Francisco, but have always lived in New York.

_____

4. He hopes to have a friend who can understand him.

_____

5. She has finished reading the history book. (把)

_____

6. If there is an opportunity, she would go to an American university.

_____

7. Since his parents work in Shanghai, they moved the family there.

_____

8. Would you lend me the math book? (把)

_____

II. Can you find the odd one out?

The words in each group are related either by meaning or by part of speech, except for one. Find the word that doesn't belong in the group.

1. 转学　　开学　　开玩笑　　借读
2. 教授　　幸运　　大学　　研究
3. 搬家　　开玩笑　　报名　　一直
4. 中文　　初中　　大学　　小学
5. 出生　　幸运　　高兴　　聪明

III. Pair Activity: Content Editor

As the class president, Maria has compiled a "Who's Who" sketchbook for the class. Below is what she wrote about Tom and Mingying. She wants you to help her make sure that the facts are accurate.

Step 1: Work individually. Based on Dialogue 1 from Lesson 1.1, decide whether Maria has got all the facts straight.

	汤姆是在美国旧金山出生的。他四岁的时候就跟父母来中国了。从小学到中学，他一直在上海国际学校上学。将来他打算上大学，可是还没有决定在美国还是在中国上大学。
	明英是在美国出生，在美国长大的。去年，她跟父母一起来到中国。她在北京第四中学学习了一年，今年转学来我们学校。她打算报名上北京大学。

Step 2: Compare your notes with your partner. Work in pairs to write Maria an email telling her if the facts are accurate.

Send	Reply	Reply All	Forward	Print	Delete

IV. Mixer Activity: What is your personal history?

Step 1: Fill out the questionnaire below for yourself. Later you will be using this information to answer your classmates' questions.

你是哪年出生的？	
你是在哪个城市出生的？	
你是在哪个城市长大的？	
你是在哪个学校上的小学？	
你是在哪个学校上的中学？	
你将来打算去哪儿上大学？	

Step 2: Pair up with a partner and complete the following interview. Record your partner's answers in the space provided.

你是哪年出生的？	
你是在哪个城市出生的？	
你是在哪个城市长大的？	
你是在哪个学校上的小学？	
你是在哪个学校上的中学？	
你将来打算去哪儿上大学？	

Step 3: Interview a third classmate. Find out who s/he just interviewed and what his/her personal history is. Record the answers in the space provided.

你采访的是谁？	
她/他是在哪儿出生的？	
她/他是在哪个城市长大的？	
她/他是在哪个学校上的小学？	
她/他将来打算去哪儿上大学？	

V. **Pair activity: What an interesting family!**

Step 1: Work individually and study the picture of the panda family below. First give each panda a Chinese name, and then write a comment about each panda below, using 多么···啊!

Model: 熊猫弟弟多么可爱啊!

1. _____

2. _____

3. _____

4. _____

5. _____

6. _____

Step 2: Pair up with a partner and share your comments with each other. If both of you have made exactly the same comment about one particular panda, write the comment below.

_____

_____

_____

_____

_____

_____

VI. **Pair Activity: Have you finished the housekeeping chores?**

Situation 1:

You and your partner are both volunteering at a senior center, working two different shifts. Before one of you gets off work, the other needs to know which housekeeping chores have been done. Be sure to use 把 as shown in the model.

Model: 问题：你把房间打扫干净了吗？

回答：打扫干净了。(Or 还没有。)

A's Sheet

Ask your partner if s/he has finished these chores. Record his/her answers.

要做的事情：	做了	需要做
1. 房间——打扫干净		
2. 衣服——洗完		
3. 厨房——打扫干净		
4. 咖啡——做好		
5. 车——洗干净		
6. 午饭——拿来		
7. 晚饭——定好		
8. 明天的活动——安排好		

B's sheet

Listen to your partner's questions and answer according to the following checklist.

要做的事情：	做了	需要做
1. 房间—打扫干净	√	
2. 衣服—洗完	√	
3. 厨房—打扫干净		√
4. 咖啡—做好		√
5. 车—洗干净	√	
6. 午饭—拿来		√
7. 晚饭—定好	√	
8. 明天的活动—安排好		√

Situation 2:

Your partner needs to be away from his/her housekeeping job today and has asked you to be a substitute. Before you get to work, you need to know which housekeeping chores have been done. Be sure to use 把 as shown in the model:

Model: 问题：你把信拿进来了吗？

回答：拿进来了。(Or 还没有。)

A's sheet

Listen to your partner's questions and answer according to the following checklist:

要做的事情：	做了	需要做
1. 信——拿进来	√	
2. 报纸——拿进来		√
3. 门窗——关好	√	
4. 衣服——洗干净		√
5. 狗——喂饱		√
6. 房间——打扫干净	√	
7. 晚饭——准备好		√
8. 狗——带出去走走	√	

B's sheet

Ask your partner if s/he has finished these chores. Record his/her answers.

要做的事情：	做了	需要做
1. 信—拿进来		
2. 报纸—拿进来		
3. 门窗—关好		
4. 衣服—洗干净		
5. 狗—喂饱		
6. 房间—打扫干净		
7. 晚饭—准备好		
8. 狗—带出去走		

VII. Group Activity: The Best Storyteller

Step 1: Pick column A or column B. Work as a group to create a short story with the words provided. Choose one representative to present your group's story in class.

A	B
十五年以前	一个月以前
去年	三个月以前
三年以前	上个星期
两年以后	昨天
小时候	两个星期以后

Step 2: Listen to each group's story. Rate the stories based on the criteria given in the next table, where 5 = excellent, 4 = good, 3 = average, 2 = weak, and 1 = poor.

	第一小组	第二小组	第三小组	第四小组
有意思 (interesting)				
有逻辑 (logical)				
有创意 (creative)				
总分 (total score)				

Step 3: Combine and average everyone's scores. The group with the highest score is the best storyteller.

VIII. Pair Activity: Mini-Dialogue

A	B
Dialogue 1 **A: You start first** • Greet B, as if s/he is a new student. • Ask B if s/he likes the school. • Ask B whether s/he takes English and Chinese courses at the same time. • Ask B which university s/he will apply to.	**B: Your partner starts first** • Greet A and tell A you just transferred here. • Tell A two things you like and one thing you don't like about the school. • Tell A you are taking both English and Chinese courses at the same time. You plan to apply to a university in the US. • Choose one university where you would like to go.
Dialogue 2 **A: Your partner starts first** • Ask B if the book is helpful. • Compliment B by using 多么···啊 (you can compliment B for being hard-working, smart, doing things fast, etc.) • Tell B you will be happy to help if s/he has questions about the exercises. • Tell B that over summer vacation, your mother made you do all the exercises in the book twice (把, 遍)	**B: You start first** • Tell A you've got a book on the college entrance exam. • Tell A you have read through the book once (把, 遍). • Tell A you haven't finished the exercises in the book because some exercises are very difficult (把). • Compliment A by using 多么···啊 (you can compliment A for being smart, helpful, kind, etc.)

IX. Meet the Author

Mr. Wang, a Chinese writer, is coming to your school to give a talk on his novels. Your teacher has given you a copy of Mr. Wang's biographical information.

Task 1: Read Mr. Wang's biography for comprehension.

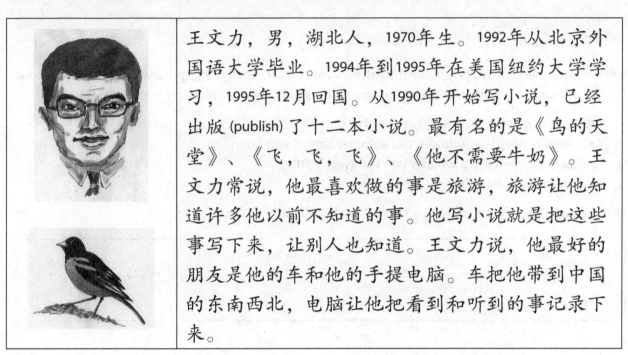

王文力，男，湖北人，1970年生。1992年从北京外国语大学毕业。1994年到1995年在美国纽约大学学习，1995年12月回国。从1990年开始写小说，已经出版 (publish) 了十二本小说。最有名的是《鸟的天堂》、《飞，飞，飞》、《他不需要牛奶》。王文力常说，他最喜欢做的事是旅游，旅游让他知道许多他以前不知道的事。他写小说就是把这些事写下来，让别人也知道。王文力说，他最好的朋友是他的车和他的手提电脑。车把他带到中国的东南西北，电脑让他把看到和听到的事记录下来。

Task 2: Write five questions based on Mr. Wang's biographical information. You can use these questions during the Q & A session following Mr. Wang's lecture.

1. _____

2. _____

3. _____

4. _____

5. _____

汉语课：＿＿＿＿＿＿＿＿＿＿＿＿ 学生姓名：＿＿＿＿＿＿＿＿＿＿＿＿

日　期：＿＿＿＿＿＿＿＿＿＿＿＿

三 · 写作练习

Create your own biography following the model of Mr. Wang's biography in Exercise IX. Your biography must be written in third person and must include the following information:

1. Your name, gender, date and place of birth
2. Your brief history (e.g. schools and summer camps you attended)
3. Your achievements (e.g. awards you received before)
4. A quote of your own or a personal motto

Note: Your biography should not exceed 200 characters.

个人小传

_____

_____

_____

_____

_____

_____

_____

1.2 竞选班长
Running for Class President

一·听力练习

I. **Match Them!**

Match the phrases you hear with the characters in Column B. Enter the corresponding numbers in Column A.

Column A 你听到的	Column B 汉字
	参加竞选
	竞选成功
	竞选助手
	竞选演讲
	社区服务
	帮助别人
	投我一票
	不能着急
	为人处事

II. **Listen to the recording of the Lesson 1.2 Dialogue first, and then answer the True/False questions in Audio Clip 1-2-2.**

	1	2	3	4
对				
错				

III. Listen to the recording of the Lesson 1.2 Text first, and then answer the True/False questions in Audio Clip 1-2-3.

	1	2	3	4	5
对					
错					

IV. Answer the questions in this section based on your understanding of Lesson 1.2.

Directions: Listen carefully to the questions in Audio Clip 1-2-4 and record your answers on an audio recorder. If you do not have a recording device, you can write down your answers below in pinyin or characters.

1. _____

   _____

2. _____

   _____

3. _____

   _____

   _____

   _____

4. _____

   _____

   _____

5. _____

   _____

   _____

6. _____

_____

_____

7. _____

_____

_____

_____

_____

V. **Rejoinders: In Audio Clip 1-2-5 you will hear five partial conversations, followed by four possible choices designated (A), (B), (C), and (D). Circle the choice that continues or completes the conversation in a logical and culturally appropriate manner.**

Note: Both the questions and the selection choices will be read only once.

1	2	3	4	5
(A)	(A)	(A)	(A)	(A)
(B)	(B)	(B)	(B)	(B)
(C)	(C)	(C)	(C)	(C)
(D)	(D)	(D)	(D)	(D)

VI. Listen to the student council election speeches (Audio Clip 1-2-6) and take notes on each candidate's qualifications.

竞选人姓名：	竞选人的优点	竞选人的经验

二·综合语言练习

I. **How do you say it in Chinese?**

1. There are three students running for class president.

_____

2. This job requires interacting with many people.

_____

3. Volunteering is a good opportunity to learn how to conduct oneself and deal with others.

_____

4. Our class president is very capable and has led our class very well.

_____

5. International students have some special needs.

_____

6. We will change this world into a more beautiful place.

_____

7. You can hang the sign at the entrance of the classroom building.

_____

8. Only by interacting more with Americans can you understand American culture.

_____

9. Only (through) understanding the students' needs can the school serve its students well.

_____

10. In addition to sports activities, we are going to organize some entertainment activities this semester.

_____

II. Did David get it right?

After hearing Maria's campaign speech (see the Lesson 1.2 Text), David sent an email to two students who were absent today. Read Maria's speech and David's email. Decide whether David's account is accurate. If not, you can jot down the discrepancies.

Send	Reply	Reply All	Forward	Print	Delete

冰冰和科文：你们好！

　　今天你们没有来参加竞选班长的活动。玛丽娅做了一个很好的演讲，我觉得她是一个非常好的候选人 (candidate)。为了让你们更了解 (understand) 她，我把她今天说的情况告诉你们一下。

　　玛丽娅最大的优点是特别能理解大家的需要。她是在意大利出生的和长大的，五岁的时候因为她爸爸妈妈到上海来工作，就搬家到上海来了。现在她每年去各国旅游。她父母在各国有很多朋友，所以她常常跟不同国家的人和文化打交道。她说，因为这样，她非常喜欢跟国际学生在一起，也特别理解大家。如果一个班长能理解我们的需要，就一定能更好地领导我们，是吧？

我们都知道她喜欢体育活动。她当了班长以后，会组织很多娱乐活动和体育活动，这些活动一定会是我们参加过的最难忘的活动。

玛丽娅还说，要在家里开一个很大的晚会，让我们都去参加。但是她没有说是这个星期还是下个星期开。等我知道了时间以后，一定告诉你们。

大卫

大卫写得对吗？如果不对，把不对的地方写下来（最少要写三个）。
1.
2.
3.
4.
5.

III. Pinyin Crossword Puzzle

Complete the pinyin crossword puzzle according to the clues given below. Your pinyin must include tones, which you should indicate by placing the numbers 1 through 4 after each pinyin syllable (for example, write neng2gan4 for nénggàn). If you get stuck, refer to the words introduced in the "Extend Your Knowledge" section of Lesson 1.2.

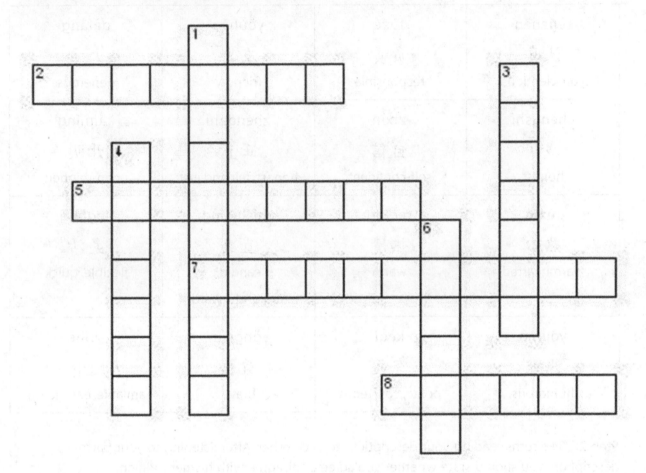

Across

2. 看见大家总是说"你好！"
5. 这样的人不会什么都怕。
7. 这样的人心里想什么就说什么。
8. 这样的人常常会说"谢谢"、"对不起"和"请问"。

Down

1. 做事很认真、很公平。
3. 很喜欢帮助别人
4. 这样的人很喜欢说笑话、开玩笑。
6. 这样的人同意做一件事就一定会把这件事做好。

IV. Pair Activity: Who fits the following description?

Step 1: Use the following words to describe a famous person and write down your descriptions in the space provided.

Please select from the following adjectives to write your descriptions:

rènzhēn 认真 conscientious	fùzé 负责 responsible	yǒuhǎo 友好 friendly	dàfāng 大方 generous
chéngshí 诚实 honest	zìxìn 自信 self-confident	zhèngzhí 正直 honest, fair and just	kāimíng 开明 open-minded
rèxīn 热心 warmhearted	rèqíng 热情 warm	zhíshuǎng 直爽 candid, straightforward	línghuó 灵活 flexible, quick
yōumò 幽默 humorous	kèqì 客气 polite, courteous	yǒnggǎn 勇敢 brave	suíhé 随和 amiable, easygoing

Step 2: Take turns reading your descriptions to each other. After listening to your partner's description, you should state whether you agree or disagree with his/her opinion.

Model: A: 玛丽娅非常聪明，又很能干。

B: 我同意。

1. _____ 同意　不同意

2. _____ 同意　不同意

3. _____ 同意　不同意

4. _____ 同意　不同意

5. _____ 同意　不同意

6. _____ 同意　不同意

7. _____ 同意　不同意

8. _____ 同意　不同意

V. **Pair Activity: What's your advice?**

Your six-year-old sister loves to ask questions like the ones in the table below. How would you and your classmates answer her questions?

Step 1: Work together with a partner to answer the following questions by using 只有…才…

Model:　问题：我怎么才能进好大学？

建议：**只有**你的高考成绩非常好**才**能进好大学。

问题	你们的建议
1. 我怎么才能有许多朋友？	
2. 将来我怎么才能当公司经理？	
3. 我怎么才能找到最好听的音乐送给我的老师？	
4. 我怎么才能让我的狗更聪明？	
5. 我将来怎么才能找到好工作？	
6. 我怎么才能参加学校的足球队？	

Step 2: Select one question from the list above and walk around the classroom to ask advice from three classmates. Record their answers in the space below.

问题：我妹妹怎么才能	？
建议 1. 只有	才能
2. 只有	才能
3. 只有	才能

Step 3: Pick the best advice and share it in class.

我的问题是：_____

我得到的最好的建议是：_____

VI. Pair Activity: Getting ready for the party!

You and your partner are setting up for a school party. You have instructions from different people on where things should be, so neither of you has a complete list. Take turns asking each other questions to make sure you have completed the tasks on the "checklist." Listen to your partner's answers and write them on the list. Use 把 in your questions and answers.

Model:　问题：我们应该把花儿放在哪儿？

　　　　　回答：我们应该把花儿放在门口。

A's Sheet

清单 (Checklist)

东西	做什么	哪儿/怎么做
花儿	放	门口
四张长桌子	放	
一张大桌子	放	教室的中间
椅子	放	
图画	挂	教室的墙上
饮料	放	
小吃	放	大桌子上
餐具	放	
客人的名字	写	本子上

B's Sheet

清单 (Checklist)

东西	做什么	哪儿/怎么做
花儿	放	门口
四张长桌子	放	教室的四边
一张大桌子	放	
椅子	放	桌子的旁边
图画	挂	
饮料	放	东边的桌子上
小吃	放	
餐具	放	大桌子上
客人的名字	写	

VII. Who is the best candidate?

Several students are running for the office of Public Relations in the Student Union. The Student Union has set up a "Face the School" website for candidates to post their qualifications. They can write no more than 100 characters to highlight their strengths.

Step 1: Read the following postings by the candidates and choose the one you would vote for.

	我叫王雪华，是高一的学生。我非常喜欢跟人打交道：同学、老师、卖东西的、开车的、做饭的、在路上走路的、认识的、不认识的…我一有空儿就跟人说话。公关 (public relations)工作太适合我了。请大家选我，谢谢！
	在我们学校，谁都认识我，谁都是我朋友。我想你们都已经认识我了，我不用再告诉你们我叫什么名字了吧？我能干、聪明、喜欢交朋友、喜欢帮助别人。我觉得我是公关天才。大家一定会选我吧？
	大家好，我是高二的张世理。我除了喜欢跟人打交道以外，还特别愿意为大家服务。每次学校开运动会、晚会、开学典礼、毕业典礼，我都来当义工。如果你们选我，我一定会好好为你们服务的。
	我叫林达，是高三的学生。我去过许多国家，特别喜欢认识跟我不一样的人。我最大的优点是能让每个人高兴，因为我知道什么话应该说，什么话不应该说。什么话应该对这个人说，不应该对那个人说。谢谢大家！

Step 2: Which candidate is the most qualified for the position? Write down the person you will vote for and use two or three sentences to justify your decision. Do not simply copy the sentences from the candidate's write-up. Instead, use your own words to summarize the candidate's qualifications.

我要选的人是：
他/她最大的优点：

Step 3: Class vote: share your decision with your class and find out which candidate receives the most votes.

VIII. Pair Activity: The Ideal Student Counselor

Suppose your school is going to recruit a new student counselor. The principal wants to hear from you what type of person you would like to work with.

Step 1: Work as individuals to fill out the questionnaire. Don't forget to cite your reasons.

学生辅导员应该	重要	不重要	为什么
1. 愿意为学生服务			
2. 愿意听学生说话			
3. 不着急			
4. 喜欢跟人打交道			
5. 有领导能力			
6. 做事又快又好			
7. 愿意帮助别人			
8. 聪明能干			
9. 理解学生的需要			
10. 能常常组织活动			

Step 2: Compare notes with your partner. Decide what three qualities are most important for a student counselor to have and write those three top qualities in the space below.

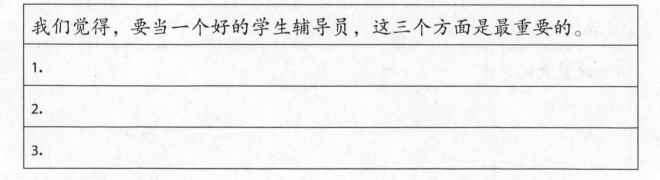

我们觉得，要当一个好的学生辅导员，这三个方面是最重要的。

1.

2.

3.

Step 3: Share your ideas in class. Your speech should begin with 我们觉得⋯

IX. **Public Speech: I recommend...**

Your Chinese teacher has asked each of you to recommend one activity that you think would make the Chinese class more interesting. What would your recommendation be? Write it down in the space given below, and then make a speech about your recommendation to your classmates. Remember, if your recommendation is well argued for, your teacher may really adopt it!

汉语课：_____   学生姓名：_____

日期：　_____

三·写作练习

Step 1: Think of one job or position that you feel you are qualified for. Write down the title of the job/position.

_____

Step 2: Use no more than 100 characters to describe your qualifications for the job/position you have listed. If extra space is needed, please use a separate piece of paper.

_____

_____

_____

_____

_____

_____

一·听力练习

I. **Match Them!**

Match the phrases you hear in Audio Clip 1-3-1 with the English phrases in Column B. Enter the corresponding numbers in Column A.

Column A 你听到的	Column B 意思
	be able to listen and understand
	be unable to understand
	be able to memorize
	be unable to play
	be able to find
	be able to hear
	be able to finish eating
	be able to study well
	be unable to see clearly
	be able to take

II. **Listen to the recording of Dialogue 1 from Lesson 1.3 first, and then answer the True/False questions in Audio Clip 1-3-2.**

	1	2	3	4	5
对					
错					

III. Listen to the recording of Dialogue 2 from Lesson 1.3 first, and then answer the True/False questions in Audio Clip 1-3-3.

	1	2	3	4	5
对					
错					

IV. Answer the questions in this section based on your understanding of Lesson 1.3.

Directions: Listen carefully to the questions in Audio Clip 1-3-4 and record your answers on an audio recorder. If you do not have a recording device, you can write down your answers below in pinyin or characters.

1. _____

2. _____

_____

_____

_____

3. _____

_____

4. _____

_____

_____

_____

5. _____

_____

_____

6. _____

V. Listen to each student talk about his/her classes in Audio Clip 1-3-5 and complete the following two tasks: (1) check off the courses they are taking this semester, and (2) indicate their favorite class using a ☺ and their least favorite class using a ☹.

		汉语	历史	数学	地理	美术	体育	化学	经济
建华	上什么课？								
	最喜欢/不喜欢								
丽美	上什么课？								
	最喜欢/不喜欢								
文静	上什么课？								
	最喜欢/不喜欢								

VI. Each statement in Audio Clip 1-3-6 describes a word introduced in Lesson 1.3. Listen to each description carefully and write down the word it refers to in the space provided. You can take notes while listening.

Model:

You will hear:	You will write:
这个词的意思是，如果我同意做一件事，我就一定会做到。	说一不二

Definition/Description Notes	Word/Phrase/Idiom
1.	
2.	
3.	
4.	
5.	
6.	

二·综合语言练习

I. **How do you say it in Chinese?**

1. If you want to change a class, you need to fill out an add/drop form.

_____

2. We need to take four required courses and two elective courses.

_____

3. You can go to the Academic Affairs Office to get the "add a course" form.

_____

4. Every week, we need to do research online.

_____

5. The teacher said we can't use cell phones for text messaging during class.

_____

6. Will you be able to memorize fifty questions tonight? (…得了)

_____

7. The geographical environment has affected the economy and culture here.

_____

8. Because the course is very boring, many students have dropped it.

_____

II. What's wrong with the history class?

Based on Dialogue 2 from Lesson 1.3, recount the problems Maria is having with her history class. Use the following paragraph outline to help you organize the story. Fill in the missing information based on your understanding of the dialogue.

这个学期除了历史课以外，玛丽娅觉得别的课都不错。教历史课的是新来的白老师。白老师讲课的时候，_____ _____。学生就做自己的事，_____ _____。白老师给的作业_____。每次的考试____ _____。因为白老师教得不好，不少学生退课了。玛丽娅没有退课，因为_____ _____。所以玛丽娅现在是进退两难。

III. Pair Activity: What is your course schedule?

Step 1: Write your course schedule for this semester.

	星期一	星期二	星期三	星期四	星期五
第一节					
第二节					
第三节					
第四节					
第五节					
第六节					

Step 2: Pair up with a partner. Ask each other questions following the suggestions given in the conversation card below. Record your partner's answers in the space provided.

对话卡

1. Find out how many required courses your partner is taking this semester.

2. Find out which electives your partner is taking besides the required courses.
   (除了……以外)

3. Find out how many electives a senior can take at your school.

4. Find out which class your partner enjoys the most and why.

5. Find out which course at your school is the most popular course and why.

IV.   **Pair Activity: Have you ever done these activities before?**

Step 1: Select nine activities from the list below to fill out your bingo board.

去中国	学法语	转学	开车
上日语课	打网球	吃月饼	迷路
背书	跟老师开玩笑	画画儿	写小说
参加竞选	退课	参加夏令营	踢足球
兼职	实习	上课发短信	做义工

Bingo Board

Step 2: Pair up with a classmate and call each other's bingo game. Take turns to ask each other questions. If your partner's answer is "I have never done this activity before" (我从来没有⋯), you can cross the activity out. Whoever crosses out three activities in a row wins the game.

Model: 问题：你上过日语课吗？

回答：上过。(Or 我从来没有上过日语课。)

V.   **What would happen to you?**

What might be the result if you ran into the following situations? Write down the possible scenarios using potential complements.

Model: 如果你给我的作业太多，_____

→   如果你给我的作业太多，我就做不完。

1. 要是我的腿没受伤，_____

2. 要是我戴了眼镜，_____

3. 要是你说话说得清楚一点儿，_____

4. 如果你让我学这么多的汉字，_____

5. 如果你给我这么多东西吃，_____

6. 要是您能少给我们一点儿功课，_____

7. 要是你能说得慢一点儿，_____

8. 如果课文里的汉字都是我认识的，_____

VI. **Mixer Activity: Who can do things the fastest?**

Using the phrases provided below, go around the class to interview three students. Write down the interviewee's name first, then ask questions about whether the student is able to accomplish a task within the given time period (see the Model below). If the student is able to accomplish the task within the given time period, put a check mark (√) under his/her name. The one who has the most check marks under their name can do things the fastest.

Model: 问题：你五分钟吃得了一个汉堡吗？

回答：吃得了。(Or 吃不了。)

时间	事情	姓名：	姓名：	姓名：
五分钟	吃一个汉堡			
两个小时	看一本书			
三分钟	跑1000米 (meter)			
半小时	做30个数学题			
十分钟	写三个电邮			
两分钟	发一条50字的短信			
一个小时	打扫你家			

做事做得最快的同学是：_____

VII.   **Pair Activity: Role Play**

Situation 1

A: You start first	B: Your partner starts first
You have just transferred to a new high school. You would like to know how to register for classes. You would also like to know how many required and elective courses you need to take a semester. What courses are required? Ask your partner for detailed information.	A newly transferred student needs detailed instructions on registering for classes. You should use phrases such as: 先⋯然后⋯，第一⋯第二⋯第三⋯. when giving information. S/he also would like to know about course requirements. Explain what and how many required and elective courses one needs to take at your school.

Situation 2

A: Your partner starts first	B: You start first
You friend is complaining about a "bad" class. Listen to his/her complaint and see if something can be done to improve the situation. When giving advice, you can use such phrases as: 你最好⋯，你为什么不⋯，我看⋯，你可以⋯，你应该⋯	You are complaining to your friend about a terrible class. Since it is already too late to drop it, you would like to get your friend's advice on how to improve the situation. Try to explain the problems specifically, so your friend can give you valuable suggestions.

VIII.   **What do they say about their teachers?**

You are visiting an online chat room and noticed that several of your friends are chatting about their teachers.

Step 1: Read what your friends have written:

平平：　我们的英语老师是个澳大利亚人，英文说得不太快，但是说得不清楚。我听了半天也没听懂多少。

飞船：　怎么会呢？是不是你的英文太差了？

快马：　不会吧。平平的英文好极了，上次他跟老外聊天，聊得可快了。英文考试也老得100分。

平平：　谢谢快马。那个澳大利亚老师看上去很老，跟我奶奶差不多。也许她说的是老人的英文，所以我们听不懂。

人爱人：会不会因为澳大利亚英文和美国英文的口音不一样？这位老太太上课有意思吗？

平平：　上课还不错，有时候给我们讲故事，有时候开玩笑，有时候还教我们唱英语歌。

快马：　这个老师挺好的。我们数学课的张老师可没意思啦。一上课他就说啊说啊，可以一直说五十分钟。

飞船：　那么厉害啊？你们多舒服啊，在下面听听，写写笔记就行了。

快马：　可是他常常是把一个问题讲了一遍又一遍，有时候一个问题要讲五六遍。好像我们什么都不懂。

人爱人：我看，你们都应该上历史课。周老师可会讲故事了，而且还常常带我们去校外参观，就是作业多。

飞船：　你说的是哪个周老师？男的还是女的？

人爱人：女的。

飞船：　要是你们上那个男的周老师的课，一定会睡觉。他一上课就让学生写汉字，每个汉字要写20遍。不写汉字的时候，就让我们背书。要是我们说话，他就把我们的名字写下来，然后报告家长。上学期我上他的汉语课，他给我妈打了八九次电话，说我不是个好学生，上课不好好学习，老说话。你们别上他的课。

Step 2: Based on their conversation, answer the following questions:

1. 同学们说到了几个老师？	
2. 这些老师教什么课？	

3. 这些老师教课教得怎么样？	
4. 如果你选课，你大概会选谁的课？	

汉语课：＿＿＿＿＿＿＿＿＿＿＿ 学生姓名：＿＿＿＿＿＿＿＿＿＿＿

日期：＿＿＿＿＿＿＿＿＿＿＿

三·写作练习

Write a short essay about your favorite class (50–100 characters). In your essay, in the space below or on a separate piece of paper, you should include:

1. General information about the course (what, when, who)
2. What do you usually do in class
3. The best part of the class

＿＿＿＿＿＿＿＿＿＿＿＿＿＿＿＿＿＿＿＿＿＿＿
＿＿＿＿＿＿＿＿＿＿＿＿＿＿＿＿＿＿＿＿＿＿＿
＿＿＿＿＿＿＿＿＿＿＿＿＿＿＿＿＿＿＿＿＿＿＿
＿＿＿＿＿＿＿＿＿＿＿＿＿＿＿＿＿＿＿＿＿＿＿
＿＿＿＿＿＿＿＿＿＿＿＿＿＿＿＿＿＿＿＿＿＿＿
＿＿＿＿＿＿＿＿＿＿＿＿＿＿＿＿＿＿＿＿＿＿＿

1.4 学生社团
Student Clubs

一 · 听力练习

I. Match Them!

Match the phrases you hear in Audio Clip 1-4-1 with the phrases you read in Column B. Enter the corresponding numbers in Column A.

Column A 你听到的	Column B 汉字
	介绍情况
	比较外向
	参加社团
	喜欢自由
	兴趣小组
	学生社团
	退出俱乐部
	分析问题
	训练时间
	轻松好玩

II. Listen to the recording of Dialogue 1 from Lesson 1.4 first, and then answer the True/False questions in Audio Clip 1-4-2.

	1	2	3	4	5
对					
错					

III. Listen to the recording of Dialogue 2 from Lesson 1.4 first, and then answer the True/False questions in Audio Clip 1-4-3.

	1	2	3	4	5
对					
错					

 IV. Answer the questions in this section based on your understanding of Lesson 1.4.

Directions: Listen carefully to the questions in Audio Clip 1-4-4 and record your answers on an audio recorder. If you do not have a recording device, you can write down your answers below in pinyin or characters.

1. _____

_____

_____

_____

_____

2. _____

_____

3. _____

_____

_____

4. _____

_____

_____

5. _____

_____

V. Audio Clip 1-4-5 includes three short listening passages. Each passage is followed by three True/False questions based on the content. After listening to each passage, circle the response that best corresponds to what you hear. Each passage will be read twice.

Passage 1

From the conversation we can infer that:

a.	The woman will continue to be part of the music group.	T	F
b.	The woman seems to want to quit the music group.	T	F
c.	The woman would like to try other extracurricular activities this semester.	T	F

Passage 2

a.	The woman wants Wei Dong to join her drama group because Wei Dong is interested in drama.	T	F
b.	Wei Dong is an extrovert and loves singing and dancing in public.	T	F
c.	Wei Dong prefers the drama club to the tennis club.	T	F

Passage 3

a.	Xiao Lin's tennis team used to train only on Fridays.	T	F
b.	Xiao Lin used to be on the national tennis team.	T	F
c.	Xiao Lin was sick last week. That is why he was not at the tennis match.	T	F

VI. Each statement in Audio Clip 1-4-6 describes a student club introduced in the "Extend Your Knowledge" section of Lesson 1.4. Listen to the descriptions and write down the name of the corresponding clubs in the space provided. You can take notes while listening.

Model:

You will hear	You will write
在这个俱乐部里，中国来的学生们在一起看电影，吃饭，开晚会，办文化活动	中国学生俱乐部

Definition/Description Notes	Name of the Student Club
1.	
2.	
3.	
4.	
5.	
6.	
7.	
8.	
9.	
10.	

二 · 综合语言练习

I. How do you say it in Chinese?

1. Student clubs will organize many interesting activities this semester.

_____

2. Since you are interested in becoming an actor, you can join the drama club.

_____

3. The computer club is planning to make a robot.

_____

4. Joining the physics club is very helpful for my studying.

_____

5. The newly-arrived baseball coach wants the baseball team to train four afternoons a week.

_____

6. Every day I need four to five hours to finish my homework, and there is no way that I will have time for student clubs.

_____

7. I can't sing or dance well. There is no way I can join the singing and dancing club.

_____

8. The international student club has activities once or twice a semester.

_____

II. Pair Activity: What is your opinion?

You and your friend are at a department store shopping for some winter clothes together. First, ask each other how to say the name of each item on display in Chinese. Then discuss whether you like the clothes on display in the "windows" below and comment on them using 又……又……

Model: 这件衣服又肥又长，多难看啊！我可不要买。

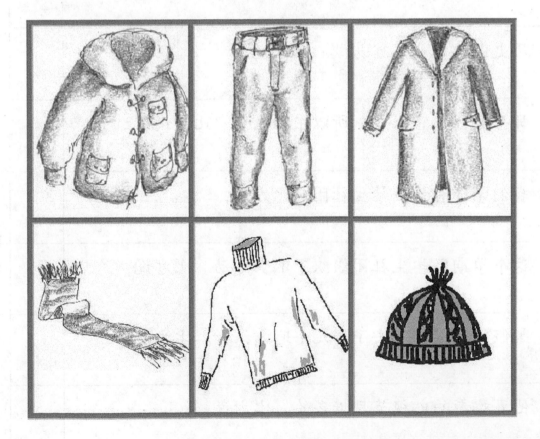

III. **Contest: Give an Example**

Divide the class into two teams. Both teams need to provide at least one example to support each statement on the list. An appropriate example is one that is concrete, such as 她演过很多电影，比方说，《活着》、《漂亮妈妈》和《风月》。An inappropriate answer is one that is too general or generic, such as 她演过很多电影，比方说，我们上课的时候看了好几个。When an appropriate example is given, the team earns 10 points. An inappropriate example costs the team 10 points. At the end of the game, tally the total points each team earns. The team that earns more points wins.

	A队	B队
1. 如果你喜欢运动，可以参加学校的运动队。比方说，		
2. 听说这个剧团演过很多有名的话剧。比方说，		
3. 数学小组的活动对学习帮助很大。比方说，		
4. 历史课的作业不容易做。比方说，		
5. 那个地方游客很多，所以东西很贵。比方说，		
6. 我们学校有许多学生社团。比方说，		
7. 这个学期，学生社团组织了不少活动。比方说，		
8. 暑假的时候，他去了好几个地方旅行。比方说，		
9. 他喜欢看的电视节目挺多的。比方说，		

10. 在美国有不少大湖。比方说，		
总分 (total score)		

IV. Pair Activity: It sounds like...

Step 1: Work individually. Write one or two sentences describing the location or organization on your list.

Model:

棒球队	棒球队每个星期训练两次。每次训练两个小时。

A's sheet

Organization/Location	Description
网球队	
熊猫饭店	
数学兴趣小组	
历史课	

B's sheet

Organization/Location	Description
戏剧社	
汉语课	
学生餐厅	
篮球队	

Step 2: Work in pairs. Take turns reading your descriptions to your partner. Listen carefully when your partner describes his/her organization or location. After your partner is finished reading his/her description, make a comment using 听上去···. To help you complete the task, you can choose words (either in positive or negative form) from the following word bank.

Model: A: 棒球队每个星期训练两次。每次训练两个小时。

  B: 听上去棒球队不太忙。

Word Bank

轻松	好玩	难	容易	多	少
有意思	忙	小	大	好	好吃
热闹	奇怪	随便	重要	特别	舒服

V. Pair Activity: It's both interesting and helpful!

Follow the instructions to finish the following dialogues.

A: **You start**	B: **Your partner starts**
• Tell B you have joined the computer club.	• Ask A what activities the computer club does.
• Tell B you learn to make web pages and animations.	• Tell A it sounds both fun and useful （有用）（又···又···）.
• Tell B you also learn to draw on the computer.	• Ask A what pictures s/he has drawn.
• Tell B you drew a panda and a dog.	• Tell A you would like to see the pictures someday.
A: **Your partner starts first**	B: **You start first**
• Ask B if the drama club is performing a play.	• Tell A you have joined the drama club.
• Ask B if s/he will play the role of the detective or the thief.	• Tell A you will perform a play about a detective and a thief.
• Tell B it sounds both difficult and interesting （又···又···）.	• Tell A you will play the role of the detective.
• Tell B you will go to see the performance.	• Tell A the drama club will perform the play next Saturday evening.

VI. Group Activity: Which club interests you most?

Various student clubs are recruiting new members. Read through the notices and choose one club that interests you. Write down the reasons why you find these clubs interesting and share what you write with your group.

Step 1: Read the following club notices.

机器人兴趣小组

同学们：

你们对机器人有兴趣吗？要是你参加机器人兴趣小组，我们可以一起研究机器人。除了研究以外，我们还可以自己做一个。比方说，我们可以替网球队做一个机器人，这样它可以帮助网球队员练习打网球。我们这个星期四下午三点半在102教室开会，欢迎你来参加！

机器人兴趣小组
9月15日

来，来，来，大家一起来跳舞！

跳舞又好玩又对健康有帮助。这个学期，跳舞队要学习拉丁(Latin)舞。你可以一边学习跳舞一边交朋友。星期三中午我们在学生餐厅开会。

跳舞队
9月13日

外国电影俱乐部

你喜欢看电影吗？喜欢看外国电影吗？想了解外国文化吗？想知道别的国家的人是怎么生活的吗？如果你的回答都是"是的"，那么你应该来参加外国电影俱乐部。我们俱乐部每个星期组织大家看一个外国电影。我们的活动又轻松又有意思。如果有兴趣，星期四晚上你可以来学校礼堂看电影。看完电影以后，你可以报名参加我们的俱乐部。

9月15日

高考数学小组

去年的数学高考让不少人非常痛苦(sad, painful)。因为做错了一两道数学题，结果就进不了好大学。进不了好大学，怎么可能找到好工作？小小的数学题影响了一个人的将来。高考数学小组一个星期活动三次，每次都练习高考难题。张老师（你们都知道她是我们学校最好的数学老师）会来给我们分析难题。我们小组最多只收十五人，如果有兴趣，你得马上来申请。可以把电邮发给：

tiancai@1098.org

20 **14** 9 71

61 $\dfrac{-b \pm \sqrt{b^2 - 4ac}}{2a}$ 58

32 41 6 18

中国武术队

武术队每星期二、四下午四点开始活动。每次活动一小时。欢迎大家报名参加。联系人：yingxiong@xyzmail.com

美食家 (Food Connoisseur)

法国面包、意大利比萨、日本饭团、中国包子、美国汉堡…这些东西你都吃过吗？

中东饭店、亚洲饭店、欧洲饭店…你都去过吗？哪个好吃？哪个不好吃？要是你参加了美食家俱乐部，我们不但可以吃到世界上最好吃的饭菜，还可以学习怎么做这些饭菜。我们每个月活动两次。一次去饭店吃饭，一次学做饭。有兴趣可以跟高三1班的马意文联系。手机：13678902741

助人为乐俱乐部

跟别的俱乐部不一样，我们俱乐部每个学期开始的时候，大家先一起决定应该帮助学校做什么，然后每个星期三下课以后，大家就一起做。要是你想把我们的学校变得更美好，让每个人都生活得更快乐，那就来参加我们的俱乐部吧。不用报名，只要星期三下午三点半来操场就行。

学校乐队

学校乐队今年要招5个队员。如果你会钢琴、小提琴、大提琴、吉他、竖琴…，请报名参加考试。考试时间：9月18日-22日。请在9月15日以前去音乐老师办公室（教室楼225室）报名。

Step 2: Choose a club and write down why you are interested in it.

我对 ＿＿＿＿＿＿＿＿＿＿＿＿＿＿＿＿＿＿ 有兴趣，因为

＿＿＿＿＿＿＿＿＿＿＿＿＿＿＿＿＿＿＿＿＿＿＿＿＿＿＿＿＿

＿＿＿＿＿＿＿＿＿＿＿＿＿＿＿＿＿＿＿＿＿＿＿＿＿＿＿＿＿

＿＿＿＿＿＿＿＿＿＿＿＿＿＿＿＿＿＿＿＿＿＿＿＿＿＿＿＿＿

＿＿＿＿＿＿＿＿＿＿＿＿＿＿＿＿＿＿＿＿＿＿＿＿＿＿＿＿＿

＿＿＿＿＿＿＿＿＿＿＿＿＿＿＿＿＿＿＿＿＿＿＿＿＿＿＿＿＿

＿＿＿＿＿＿＿＿＿＿＿＿＿＿＿＿＿＿＿＿＿＿＿＿＿＿＿＿＿

＿＿＿＿＿＿＿＿＿＿＿＿＿＿＿＿＿＿＿＿＿＿＿＿＿＿＿＿＿

＿＿＿＿＿＿＿＿＿＿＿＿＿＿＿＿＿＿＿＿＿＿＿＿＿＿＿＿＿

VII. Student Club Poster Competition

Task:

Imagine that you would like to start a student club at your school. What would this club be? Who could join your club? What kind of activities would your club organize? Why should your classmates join your club? What would be your club mascot/symbol/T-shirt design? Make a poster advertising your club. Your poster should meet the following criteria:

1. The name and the description of your club must be appealing to your fellow students.
2. Proofread your poster before posting it in class.
3. Your poster should be artistically appealing.
4. To ensure a fair competition, do not write your name on the poster.

Once you finish making your poster, display it at the designated place in your classroom.

Competition Procedures:

The competition can be organized by the class president or the teacher.

1. Assign a number to each poster.
2. Make copies of the poster evaluation handout and distribute them to students.
3. Ask students to vote for the best poster. Students must give reasons for why they think one poster is better than the other ones.

Evaluation Handout:

广告号码：_____	俱乐部名：_____	
1 ---------------- 10 不好-----------非常好	广告内容：	
	俱乐部的名字很吸引人。	
	俱乐部的活动很有意思。	
	参加俱乐部的学生很多样。	
	俱乐部的活动时间比较合适。	
	俱乐部的会标/T-恤衫很漂亮。	

广告号码：_____	俱乐部名：_____	
1 ---------------- 10 不好-----------非常好	广告内容：	
	俱乐部的名字很吸引人。	
	俱乐部的活动很有意思。	
	参加俱乐部的学生很多样。	
	俱乐部的活动时间比较合适。	
	俱乐部的会标/T-恤衫很漂亮。	

广告号码：＿＿＿＿＿＿	俱乐部名：＿＿＿＿＿＿＿＿＿＿＿＿＿＿	
1 —————— 10 不好————非常好	广告内容：	
	俱乐部的名字很吸引人。	
	俱乐部的活动很有意思。	
	参加俱乐部的学生很多样。	
	俱乐部的活动时间比较合适。	
	俱乐部的会标/T-恤衫很漂亮。	

汉语课：＿＿＿＿＿＿＿＿＿＿ 学生姓名：＿＿＿＿＿＿＿＿＿＿＿

日期：＿＿＿＿＿＿＿＿＿＿

三·写作练习

Write a paragraph (50–100 characters) describing the extracurricular activities that you are participating in this semester. In the paragraph, you need to state which student clubs or sports teams you have joined and the reasons you have chosen these activities. If you have not joined any clubs or sports teams, you can talk about the activities you usually do after class. Give explanations for why you like to do these activities. If extra space is needed, please use a separate piece of paper.

1.5 开班会
Holding a Class Meeting

一·听力练习

I. Match Them!

Match the phrases you hear in Audio Clip 1-5-1 with the phrases you read in Column B. Enter the corresponding numbers in Column A.

Column A 你听到的	Column B 汉字
	关于健康的问题
	关于作业的问题
	关于饮食文化
	关于美国文化讲座
	关于学生社团
	关于中国的现代画
	关于运动和健康的问题
	关于中国经济的讲座

II. Listen to the recording of Dialogue 1 from Lesson 1.5 first, and answer then the True/False questions in Audio Clip 1-5-2.

	1	2	3	4
对				
错				

III. Listen to the recording of Dialogue 2 from Lesson 1.5 first, and then answer the True/False questions in Audio Clip 1-5-3.

	1	2	3	4
对				
错				

IV. Answer the questions in this section based on your understanding of Lesson 1.5.

Directions: Listen carefully to the questions in Audio Clip 1-5-4 and record your answers on an audio recorder. If you do not have a recording device, you can write down your answers below in pinyin or characters.

1. _____

_____

2. _____

_____

_____

3. _____

_____

_____

4. _____

_____

_____

V. Rejoinders: In Audio Clip 1-5-5 you will hear five partial conversations, each followed by four possible choices designated (A), (B), (C), and (D). Circle the choice that continues or completes the conversation in a logical and culturally appropriate manner.

Note: Both the questions and the choices will be read only once.

1	2	3	4	5
(A)	(A)	(A)	(A)	(A)
(B)	(B)	(B)	(B)	(B)
(C)	(C)	(C)	(C)	(C)
(D)	(D)	(D)	(D)	(D)

VI. Each statement in Audio Clip 1-5-6 describes a phrase or idiom that you learned in your second year of study. First, refresh your memory and review the meanings and usages of the phrases in the word bank below. Afterwards listen to each description carefully and write down the phrase it refers to in the space provided. You can take notes while listening.

Model:

You will hear	You will write:
这个俗语的意思是，花了很大的力气做一件事情。	九牛二虎之力

Word Bank

种瓜得瓜，种豆得豆	酒肉朋友
喝西北风	读万卷书，行万里路
一分钱一分货	不怕不识货，就怕货比货
好货不便宜，便宜没好货	病从口入，祸从口出
浪子回头金不换	一寸光阴一寸金

Definition/Description Notes	Proverbs:
1.	
2.	
3.	
4.	
5.	
6.	
7.	
8.	
9.	
10.	

二·综合语言练习

I. **How do you say it in Chinese?**

1. Every day I spend six to seven hours doing homework. Studying is too stressful.

_____

2. Why are you always complaining about the chemistry class?

_____

3. Every time after she finishes the homework, she checks it three or four times.

_____

4. Because students have different learning approaches (methods), a teacher should not use only one approach in teaching.

_____

5. The time when the Chinese culture lectures are held is on the first Wednesday of every month.

_____

6. This month's Chinese culture lecture is about Chinese modern arts.

_____

7. Is this topic very interesting?

_____

8. In order to help students prepare for the college entrance examination, Teacher Wang feels the more homework there is, the better.

_____

9. The Chinese student speaks English very well, s/he sounds like an American.

_____

10. During the class meeting, they discussed different learning approaches.

_____

II. Meeting Notes

When the class had its meeting (see Dialogues 1 and 2 from Lesson 1.5), Mingying took some notes. Compare the notes with the dialogues. Did Mingying take accurate notes? If not, write the discrepancies in the table below.

班会笔记

日期： 9月20日 参加人： 全班同学

讨论题目：

1. 作业

大家的意见不同。有的觉得作业太多，要六七个小时才能做完。有的觉得作业太少，两三个小时就做完了，做完以后，有很多时间参加别的活动。有的觉得作业不多不少，三四个小时可以做完。班长说，作业做完以后最好要检查三四遍。

---

2. 中国文化讲座

这个学期有四个讲座，时间是每个月第一个星期一的下午四点。有四个话题，可是大家都不喜欢第四个话题，因为都是讲给老年人听的。大家决定要请一个法国人来谈谈北京的中小学，还要请一个音乐学院的学生来谈谈弹钢琴和唱歌。

明英的班会笔记都写得对吗？有哪些地方不对？
1.
2.
3.
4.
5.

III. Mixer Activity: We have some advice for you…

Your school has a peer coaching website, where students can pose their questions or problems and get advice from their fellow students.

Step 1: Work individually. Choose 3–4 questions/problems from the following log and write your advice in the space provided. Your advice must incorporate the expression 不就可以…了吗？

Model: 问题：我每次做汉语作业都做得很慢，因为我写汉字写得太慢了。

建议：要是你用电脑打字，**不就可以**快一点儿做完汉语作业**了吗**？

学生姓名	问题	建议
白汉明	我每次数学考试都会把题做错，从来没有得过100分。我应该怎么提高数学考试的成绩？	
张卫	有一个女生很喜欢我，请我跟她一起去看电影，可是我不喜欢她。应该怎么办？	
钱文红	我非常想参加学校棒球队，可是教练说我打棒球打得不够好，不能参加校队。大家有什么建议？	
丁雨林	英语课的老师要我们一天背二三十个词，我总是今天背了，明天就忘了。怎么才能不忘呢？	
林丽丽	我很想看外国电影。哪儿可以看到最新的外国电影？	
杰米	每次我做作业的时候，我的猫就来跟我玩儿。它总是坐在我的书上或作业本上，不让我写字看书。	
大卫	老师要我们寒假看三本汉语小说。可是这些小说里边有很多我不认识的汉字，怎么看得完呢？	
马克	谁知道哪儿有卖便宜的滑板吗？	

金业中	我想把一些旧课本卖了，你们知道怎么卖吗？	
玛丽	我非常想去美国的东北部旅行，可是我父母不放心我一个人去。有什么建议吗？	

Step 2: Walk around the class to find solutions to 3–4 of the questions/problems that you haven't given advice to. Listen to your classmates' suggestions and record the essential information in the log. You should have 6–8 entries on the list total.

Step 3: Take turns to report the advice offered for every question/problem. Listen to your classmates carefully and complete the entire list.

IV. Pair Activity: So, you are interested in…

You and your partner are comparing notes on the activities you did lately. You would like to know more details about the activities your partner did.

Step 1: Choose one topic that you are interested in (it can be real or imagined). Do not let your partner know which topic you have chosen. Based on the topic, write out the details about your recent activities in the space provided.

体育	法国	宠物	汉语	历史
饮食	经济	中国	美国	数学
音乐	艺术	电脑	高考	旅游

A's Sheet

活动	关于
看了一个电影	
看了一本小说	
去了博物馆	
听了一个讲座	

B's Sheet

活动	关于
听了一个报告	
看了一本书	
去了一个讨论会	
去了夏令营	

Step 2: Take turns asking questions. Listen to your partner's answers carefully and decide which topic s/he is interested in. When answering questions, use 关于 in your answers.

Model: 你最近做什么了？

我看了一个关于熊猫的电影。

My partner is interested in:

体育	法国	宠物	汉语	历史
饮食	经济	中国	美国	数学
音乐	艺术	电脑	高考	旅游

V. Pair Activity: What do we have in common?

Step 1: Work as individuals. Complete the statements in the column of 我觉得 according to your preference. Do not let your partner see your answers.

我觉得	你觉得
1. 作业越 _____ 越好。	1. 作业越 _____ 越好。
2. 汉语说得越快越 _____。	2. 汉语说得越快越 _____。
3. 越有钱的人越 _____。	3. 越有钱的人越 _____。
4. 她的猫越 _____ 越 _____。	4. 她的猫越 _____ 越 _____。

Step 2: Take turns to ask questions. Record your partner's answers in the column of 你觉得.

Model: 你觉得她的猫越跑越快吗？

是的。(Or 不，我觉得她的猫越吃越胖。)

Step 3: Check whether you and your partner have the same opinion on any of the statements. If you agree on all of them, you've found someone who thinks like you.

VI. **Group Activity: Are you satisfied?**

Your school is conducting a survey to determine areas for improvement. Students are encouraged to complain about the school's services and classes they don't like. Work in groups of three or four. First decide, as a group, which service or class you feel needs the most improvement. Explain what the problem is by giving detailed examples. Then propose a few possible solutions to the problem. Assign one group member as the note taker to fill out the following survey form.

关于：_____

大家的抱怨：

1.

2.

3.

4.

5.

6.

7.

8.

大家的建议：

1.

2.

3.

4.

VII. **You've got mail!**

Send	Reply	Reply All	Forward	Print	Delete

　　今天汤姆告诉我，这个星期五下午五点半在社区广场有一个讲座。听说来演讲的是一位有名的艺术家，丁歌先生。汤姆说，这位丁先生是天才，除了画画儿以外，他还写过不少流行歌和三本小说。丁歌先生最有名的歌叫《我爱你我他》。你听过吗？我没听过。汤姆也没听过，可是他说在"丁歌，我们爱你"的网站可以免费下载。

　　现在丁先生还开了一家唱片公司、一个衣服店、和一个小小的艺术博物馆。唱片公司做的是丁歌唱片，衣服店卖的是丁歌牌的衣服和鞋子，艺术博物馆里有丁先生的画儿。

　　汤姆还说，丁先生当过体操运动员、体育教练、老师、公司经理，做过许多不同的工作，比方说在饭店做饭，在商店卖东西，在搬家公司帮人搬家，在博物馆卖票，在飞机上当服务员等等。丁先生已经会说八种外语，现在正在学习第九种－意大利语，因为他要学唱意大利歌剧(opera)。

　　我觉得这位丁先生很不一般。你见过会做那么多事的人吗？因为不知道汤姆说的是不是真的，所以我想去听听丁先生的讲座，然后当面(in person)问问他，他是不是真的那么聪明能干。星期五如果你有空儿，跟我一起去，好吗？

明乐

丁歌先生

Task 1: What is the essential information you got from this email?

谁 (who)?	
什么时候 (when)?	
哪儿 (where)?	
什么 (what)?	

Task 2: Suppose you are going to Mr. Ding's lecture. Write five questions for the question and answer session.

1)	
2)	
3)	
4)	
5)	

VIII. **Pair Activity: Mini-Interview**

Step 1: Work individually. Write answers to the following questions, based on your own situation.

1. 你每天做作业要花多少时间？

2. 哪门课的作业最多？哪门课的作业最难？

3. 做完作业以后，你检查一遍吗？

4. 你觉得高中生每天应该花多长时间做功课？为什么？

5. 有些同学觉得，老师给学生的功课越少越好。你同意吗？为什么？

Step 2: Interview each other by asking the same questions. Use the answers you've prepared to answer your partner's questions. When it is your partner's turn to respond, listen and take notes.

1. 你每天做作业要花多少时间？

2. 哪门课的作业最多？哪门课的作业最难？

3. 做完作业以后，你检查一遍吗？

4. 你觉得高中生每天应该花多长时间做功课？为什么？

5. 有些同学觉得，老师给学生的功课越少越好。你同意吗？为什么？

IX. If I organized a lecture...

Prepare to give a speech in class on the topic "If I Organized a Lecture." In your speech, tell your classmates what lecture you would organize and why. If everybody in your class is interested in the lecture, brainstorm how to make it a reality.

汉语课：＿＿＿＿＿＿＿＿＿＿＿　　　学生姓名：＿＿＿＿＿＿＿＿＿＿＿

日期：＿＿＿＿＿＿＿＿＿＿＿

三·写作练习

Write an article describing your favorite elementary school teacher. Your description cannot exceed 200 characters. It must include the following information:

1. The teacher's name and the subjects he/she teaches
2. The teacher's brief history: e.g. how long he/she has been teaching, etc.
3. The teacher's accomplishments
4. Why do you like this teacher?

我最喜欢的小学老师

＿＿＿＿＿＿＿＿＿＿＿＿＿＿＿＿＿＿＿＿＿＿＿＿＿＿＿＿＿＿

＿＿＿＿＿＿＿＿＿＿＿＿＿＿＿＿＿＿＿＿＿＿＿＿＿＿＿＿＿＿

＿＿＿＿＿＿＿＿＿＿＿＿＿＿＿＿＿＿＿＿＿＿＿＿＿＿＿＿＿＿

＿＿＿＿＿＿＿＿＿＿＿＿＿＿＿＿＿＿＿＿＿＿＿＿＿＿＿＿＿＿

＿＿＿＿＿＿＿＿＿＿＿＿＿＿＿＿＿＿＿＿＿＿＿＿＿＿＿＿＿＿

＿＿＿＿＿＿＿＿＿＿＿＿＿＿＿＿＿＿＿＿＿＿＿＿＿＿＿＿＿＿

＿＿＿＿＿＿＿＿＿＿＿＿＿＿＿＿＿＿＿＿＿＿＿＿＿＿＿＿＿＿

＿＿＿＿＿＿＿＿＿＿＿＿＿＿＿＿＿＿＿＿＿＿＿＿＿＿＿＿＿＿

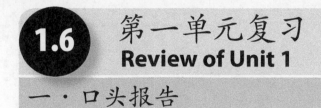

一·口头报告

Choose one of the topics from the list below to give an oral presentation in class. Your presentation must meet the following criteria:

1. It must have a beginning, a middle, and an end.
2. It must include as much detail as possible.
3. It must last no longer than two minutes.

After you have chosen the topic, please write an outline for your presentation. You can write the outline on a separate sheet of paper. If your teacher allows, you can also transfer the outline to an index card as a reminder when you give the presentation.

Topic 1. 我将来想上的大学

Topic 2. 我最喜欢做的社区服务

Topic 3. 我最喜欢上的课

Topic 4. 我最喜欢的学生社团

Topic 5. 我希望参加的文化讲座

Topic 6. 为什么参加学生社团很重要？

Topic 7. 高中生参加运动队会不会影响学习？

Topic 8. 我们为什么要了解不同国家的文化？

二·综合语言练习

I. **Did Grandma get it right?**

After Grandma read Tom's email (see the Lesson 1.6 Text), she told Grandpa about it. Based on Tom's email, decide whether Grandma got all the facts right.

Grandma's account:

奶奶说：	对	不对
1. 汤姆想知道爷爷是不是已经会用电脑打字了。		
2. 汤姆这个学期跟上个学期差不多忙。		
3. 因为汤姆明年就要高考了，所以老师给的作业很多。		
4. 汤姆每天做作业要三四个小时，可是有的学生要六七个小时。		
5. 汤姆这个学期学了四门课。		
6. 汤姆最喜欢上数学课了，因为数学老师的教学方法特别好。		
7. 除了上课以外，汤姆没有时间参加学生社团的活动。		
8. 汤姆每个周末都去一个老人组织做义工。		
9. 暑假的时候，汤姆就在那个老人组织工作过。		
10. 汤姆说杰米要把他的秘密写信告诉爷爷奶奶。		

II. The Story of Xiao Gao

Based on the Lesson 1.6 Dialogue, compile the story of Xiao Gao. Use the following paragraph outline to help you organize the story. Fill in the missing information based on your understanding of the dialogue.

小高是_____的孩子。他出生以后，_____
不能去幼儿园，他父母的工作又很忙，所以_____。
他就跟张奶奶的孩子一样。长大以后，小高常常来看张奶奶。现在_____
_____。高中毕业以后，他_____。

Now, it's your turn to write a short paragraph about Xiao Gao's life in high school. You can write about his studies, his hobbies, his friends, or his life in general. After you have finished your story, share it with your classmates.

III. **Pair Activity: Do you know any of them?**

Both of you are planning to attend a class for students with special talents. Today you've gotten a list of the students who have already registered for the class. It happens that both of you already know some people on the list. Select two people from the list and tell your partner about him/her in 3–5 sentences. While your partner speaks, make a note of what they say. Afterwards, you can compare notes to see if you got the facts right.

	马克
	汉姆

	高通运
	玛丽
	白建方
	丁越星
	山姆
	林百英

IV. Board Game

Use the words provided on each line to form a sentence. Write down your sentences. The first one (or team) to reach FINISH and get all sentences correct wins the game.

把	做完	我	晚上	要	今天	作业	▼
							▼
一遍	请	把	你	书	再	这本	看	▼
							▼
学生的	张老师	特别	需要	理解			▼
							▼
又	又	聪明	我们的	能干	班长		▼
							▼
身体	才	努力	只有	能	学习	健康	▼
							▼
把	更	我们	世界	美好	要	变得	▼
							▼
的	的	高考	关于	是	讲座	今天	▼
							▼
							FINISH

V. Group Activity: Teacher of the Year

Your school is asking you to vote for "Teacher of the Year".

Step 1: Read the candidates' achievements, and vote for the best teacher.

高卫老师	高老师一直教初三的数学课。他工作认真，关心学生，热心地为学生服务。为了让学生考上重点高中，高老师不但每天给学生很多作业，而且还建立了一个"有难题就找高老师"的网站，专门为学生分析难题。去年，高老师教的学生都考进了高中，还有24个学生考进了重点高中。
黄小丽老师	黄老师大学一毕业就到我们学校来教书。她工作认真负责，对学生非常友好，也特别愿意帮助学生。每天晚上，黄老师都在学校帮助学生学习。她还经常带学生去不同的地方参观，让大家不但能从课本上，而且能从社会上学到新知识。
钱雪明老师	钱老师教学有十多年的历史了。她不但帮助学生，而且帮助新老师学习怎么教书。钱老师觉得，一个好老师应该理解学生的需要和兴趣。只有这样，才能把学生教好。为了了解学生，她每个周末都去学生家跟学生和学生家长谈话。她还用自己的钱买了很多书和词典送给学生。学生都说，她就像他们的妈妈一样。
张元航老师	常常有学生抱怨说，张老师的课太难了。张老师对学生很严，每天都让学生看书，还要做作业。他的作业不容易，需要学生上网研究。但是上过张老师课的学生都说，上课的时候觉得难，上完了以后觉得学到了很多知识。张老师教过的高三学生，差不多都考进了大学。有的还去国外上大学。

Step 2: Tally all of your classmates' votes. The teacher with the most votes is "Teacher of the Year."

VI. Pair Activity: Where did Buddy hide the slipper?

Step 1: Buddy, Grandpa Wang's dog, loves to hide his slippers. Choose three possibilities from the pictures below and write three sentences, using 把…带到/放到/放在（地方）.

Model: 八弟可能把拖鞋带到外面去了。

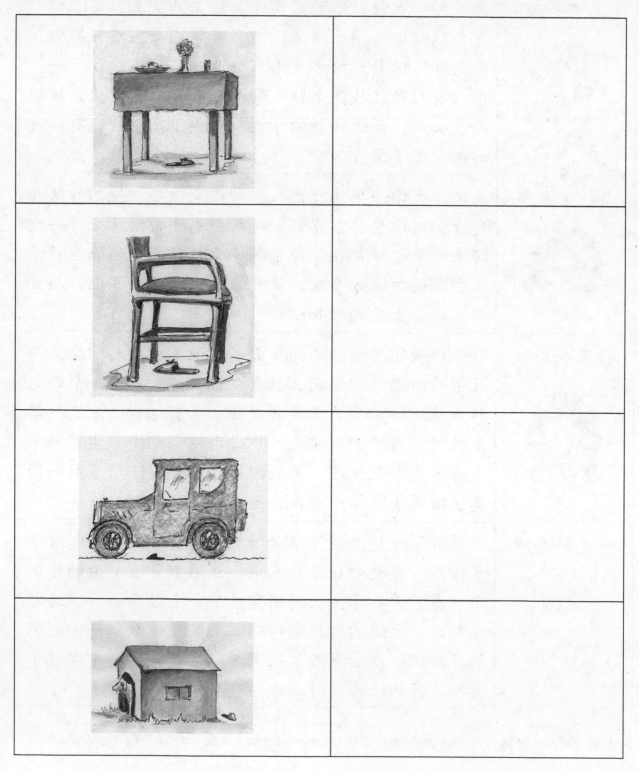

Step 2: Pair up with a partner. See what the other person sees as possibilities.

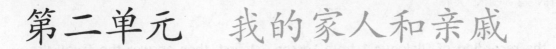

第二单元　我的家人和亲戚

UNIT 2　My Family and Relatives

2.1　姥姥和姥爷
Grandma and Grandpa

一・听力练习

I. **Match Them!**

Match the phrases you hear in Audio Clip 2-1-1 with the English phrases in Column B. Enter the corresponding numbers in Column A.

Column A 你听到的	Column B 意思
	bring back (towards)
	move up (away)
	walk into (towards)
	fly out (away)
	kick over (towards)
	lift up
	put down (away)
	sit down (towards)
	put back (away)
	bring up (towards)

II. Listen to the recording of Dialogue 1 from Lesson 2.1 first, then answer the True/False questions in Audio Clip 2-1-2.

	1	2	3	4	5
对					
错					

III. Listen to the recording of Dialogue 2 from Lesson 2.1 first, and then answer the True/False questions in Audio Clip 2-1-3.

	1	2	3	4	5
对					
错					

IV. Answer the questions in this section based on your understanding of the Lesson 2.1 dialogues.

Directions: Listen carefully to the questions in Audio Clip 2-1-4 and record your answers on an audio recorder. If you do not have a recording device, you can write down your answers below in pinyin or characters.

1. _____

_____

_____

2. _____

_____

_____

3. _____

_____

_____

_____

_____

4. _____

_____

5. _____

_____

_____

_____

V. Rejoinders: In Audio Clip 2-1-5 you will hear five partial conversations, each followed by four possible choices designated (A), (B), (C), and (D). Circle the letter for the choice that continues or completes the conversation in a logical and culturally appropriate manner.

Note: Both the questions and the choices will be read once.

1	2	3	4	5
(A)	(A)	(A)	(A)	(A)
(B)	(B)	(B)	(B)	(B)
(C)	(C)	(C)	(C)	(C)
(D)	(D)	(D)	(D)	(D)

VI. Each statement in Audio Clip 2-1-6 describes a Chinese term for an extended family member. These terms were introduced in "你知道吗？" section of your textbook. Listen to the descriptions carefully and write down the corresponding term in the space provided. You can take notes while listening.

Model:

You will hear:	You will write:
这个词的意思是爸爸的姐姐或者妹妹。	姑姑 (gūgu)

Definition/Description Notes	Name of the Student Club:
1.	
2.	
3.	
4.	
5.	
6.	
7.	
8.	

二·综合语言练习

I. How do you say it in Chinese?

1. Yesterday, I went to a banquet to celebrate my parents' 20th wedding anniversary.

_____

2. Most (more than half) of our (family's) relatives live in Beijing.

_____

3. My parents won't let me date in high school.

_____

4. My parents said they had become good friends in high school.

_____

5. In China, only men above 22 years old can get married.

_____

6. My father married my mother when he was 23 years old.

_____

7. I don't think dating will affect studies.

_____

8. Many students do not devote their whole heart when they are dating.

_____

II. **Pair Activity: Who came to the banquet?**

At his grandparents' request, Tom prepared a "guest list" for those relatives who might attend his grandparents' 40th wedding anniversary banquet. Some came and some didn't. Based on Dialogue 1 in Lesson 2.1, help Tom to check off the list of relatives who attended. Then add up the total number of attendees. After you have finished, compare notes with your partner. If there is any difference, try to resolve it.

这些亲戚会来参加姥姥姥爷结婚四十周年的酒席：	来了
姥姥姥爷	
我们家4人（爸爸、妈妈、杰米和我）	
舅姥爷一家8人（姥姥的兄弟）（住在南京）	
大姥姨一家10人（姥姥的姐姐）（住在上海）	
小姥姨一家5人（姥姥的妹妹）（住在上海）	
大姥爷一家23人（姥爷的大哥）（住在重庆）	
二姥爷一家11人（姥爷的二哥）（住在上海）	
四姥爷一家12人（姥爷的弟弟）（住在上海）	
大姑姥姥一家9人（姥爷的姐姐）（住在广州）	
小姑姥姥一家15人（姥爷的妹妹）（住在上海）	
小舅舅一家3人（住在上海）	
大舅舅一家3人（住在上海）	
来参加酒席的亲戚一共有：	

III. A Love Story

Based on Dialogue 2 from Lesson 2.1, rearrange the following sentences into a chronological love story for Tom's grandparents. You need to use all of the "time words" in the table below in your story. These time words can be used more than once.

Time words:

那时候	后来	以后	四十多年以前	又过了两年

1. 姥姥和姥爷在一个学校上高中。
2. 他们从高中毕业了。
3. 他们开始谈恋爱。
4. 他们结婚以后，姥姥搬家去北京了。
5. 他们都参加了学校的合唱团，成了好朋友。
6. 姥姥在上海一个幼儿园当老师，姥爷去北京上大学了。
7. 姥爷大学毕业了。
8. 姥姥姥爷互相写信。
9. 姥姥姥爷结婚了。

IV. Pair Activity: Dog Training

You and your partner both volunteer at "Dogs for the Disabled." The dog trainer is having a hard time training a few "slow learners" to do certain things.

Step 1: Read the profiles of these "slow learners"

狗的情况 (Dog Profile)	
帮帮	• 帮帮喜欢跑来跑去，不愿意在一个地方。 • 它很喜欢不同的颜色。如果一个地方有很多颜色，它就愿意在那里看来看去。
点点	• 点点非常喜欢睡觉。可是因为它非常喜欢跟人去外边走路，一听到开门的声音，马上就会起来。 • 点点也喜欢看电视，特别是看卡通片。但是如果卡通片里有狗，它就会汪汪地叫。
大王	• 大王吃得太多了，看到吃的东西就不想离开。 • 大王非常喜欢音乐，听到了音乐，就会跟着音乐一边叫一边跳舞。
能能	• 能能一看到自行车就很高兴，它会不停地叫。 • 它喜欢下雨天，听到水的声音就会安静地坐下来。
三弟	• 三弟不注意听别人的话。可是你多说几次，它还是会听你。 • 三弟非常喜欢跟小孩子在一起玩。
朋朋	• 朋朋总是想出去玩，已经自己跑出去好几次，还迷了两次路。 • 它不喜欢红颜色。如果看到穿红衣服的人，就会跑回来。

Step 2: Based on the profiles, work with your partner to offer suggestions for the dog trainer. Be sure to write your suggestions using 只要···就···

Model: 只要不让点点看有狗的卡通片，它就不会叫了。

姓名	需要学会	你们的建议 (Answers may vary.)
帮帮	停在一个地方	
点点	少睡觉	
大王	少吃一点儿	
能能	看到自行车不叫	
三弟	听别人的话	
朋朋	不跑出去玩儿	

V. Mixer Activity: The School's "Open House"

You are all serving on the organizing committee for your school's "Open House." As the last step of the preparation, you need to set up the "Open House" location and make sure that everything is in its right place.

Step 1: Glance through the left column of the "task list" below and select two tasks from the list that you "have completed." Write your name next to the task in the right column.

要做的事情	谁做的？
1) 桌子→搬出去	
2) 椅子→搬进来	
3) 图片→挂上去	
4) 牌子→拿下来	
5) 花→放出去	
6) 点心→拿进来	
7) 饮料→拿过去	
8) 通知→挂起来	
9) 音乐光盘→拿过去	
10) 笔→拿进来	
11) 餐巾纸→拿过来	
12) 电脑→搬上来	

Step 2: Walk around the classroom and ask 3–5 students whether they have finished the tasks that you haven't done. You can ask each student only one question. Write their names next to the tasks they have done.

Model:　你：　　　你把桌子搬**出去**了吗？

　　　　　　你同学：搬**出去**了。(Or 我没有搬**出去**。)

Step 3: See who has a complete task list.

VI. Group Activity: What's your story?

Step 1: Work in groups of three or four. The following table has the first line of four stories. Everyone in the group should pick one line and write a sentence to continue the story. After you have finished your sentence, pass the story on to the student sitting next to you. S/he will write the next sentence. Go around the group until the story is finished. Each story should have 5–10 sentences and use 以后 or 后来 at least once.

三十多年以前，爸爸在幼儿园认识了妈妈。
高中毕业以后，他打算离开家。
那只猫是姥姥在菜场找到的。
山姆参加了学校的合唱队。

Step 2: Share the finished stories with your group and vote for the best story to be shared with your class.

Note: Your conversation must be carried out in Chinese!

Step 3: Each group shares the best story with the class.

VII. Why was Jim unhappy?

Send	Reply	Reply All	Forward	Print	Delete

爷爷：您好！

上个星期天，我们去美心酒家参加了姥姥姥爷结婚四十周年的酒席。妈妈说，因为有许多亲戚朋友要来，所以我应该穿得漂亮一点儿。我决定穿那件我最喜欢的，现在最流行的衣服，可是妈妈一见就叫起来："不行，不行。我们去参加一个喜庆的酒席，你怎么能穿这种衣服呢？"她非要我换一件。我不知道我的衣服有什么不对。那是一件白色的衣服，上面有一个骷髅 (kūlú, skeleton) 头像。这种衣服现在很酷啊，我有好几个同学都穿这种衣服，有的还穿有骷髅头的鞋子呢。妈妈给我找了一件白衬衣和一条黑裤子。我觉得只有饭店的服务员才穿那样的衣服，可是妈妈不听我的，非要我穿。这让我很不高兴。

那天，来了许多亲戚朋友，可是来的人多数我都不认识。有很多老人，是姥姥姥爷的兄弟姐妹，或者是他们在上海的老朋友。这些老人一直在说上海话，我听不懂。爸爸妈妈让我和汤姆"叫人" (address people by their titles)。可是我不知道叫他们什么。我叫年纪大的男人爷爷，年纪大的女人奶奶。可是妈妈说我叫错了。有的要叫姑姥姥，有的要叫舅姥爷……我一点儿也记不住。不少老人看到我就叫我"小弟弟"。这不是很奇怪吗？我不是他们的小弟弟啊。

后来我们开始吃饭。有八个冷菜、八个热菜，还有汤和甜点心。那些亲戚们总是让我多吃一点儿。我说我已经吃饱了，不想再吃了，可是他们说："你怎么那么客气？"他们把很多很多菜放到我的盘子里，有些菜是我不爱吃的。我觉得要是我想吃什么，自己会拿，不用他们帮我拿。可是爸爸听了我的抱怨以后，说我不懂中国文化。

爷爷，你能告诉我，我哪儿做错了吗？

杰米

Based on Jim's email, list at least three of the things that made Jim somewhat unhappy:

VIII. What's your opinion?

In the email you read for Activity VII, Jim complained about certain Chinese ways of doing things. Do you know why the Chinese do things this way? Choose the answer that you believe is the reason.

1. 中国人觉得喜庆的时候不能穿带骷颅头的衣服，因为
   a. 中国人觉得骷颅头不传统。
   b. 中国人觉得骷颅头不好看。
   c. 中国人觉得骷颅头不吉利 (jílì, lucky)。
   d. 中国人觉得骷颅头不够酷。

2. 在中国学会"叫人"很重要，因为
   a. 中国人很注意人跟人的关系。
   b. 中国人觉得不会叫人就是说汉语说得不好。
   c. 中国人喜欢跟不同的人在一起。
   d. 中国的老人喜欢别人客气地称呼 (chēnghū, address) 他们。

3. 在酒席上，中国人常常让别人多吃一点儿，因为
   a. 中国人喜欢大家都长得胖一点。
   b. 中国人觉得这样做很客气。
   c. 中国人喜欢大吃大喝。
   d. 酒席上的菜太多了，中国人要把菜都吃完。

汉语课：＿＿＿＿＿＿＿＿＿＿＿　　学生姓名：＿＿＿＿＿＿＿＿＿＿＿

日期：　　＿＿＿＿＿＿＿＿＿＿＿

三・写作练习

Interview your family members, neighbors, or friends about how they met each other and got married. Write a story based on your interview. Your story must have a title, such as "(一个人的名字)的爱情故事," and must contain at least 200 characters. If extra space is needed, please use a separate piece of paper.

2.2

独生子女
The Only Child

一 · 听力练习

I. **Match Them!**

Match the phrases you hear in Audio Clip 2-2-1 with the phrases you read in Column B. Enter the corresponding numbers in Column A.

Column A 你听到的	Column B 汉字
	网上聊天
	独生子女
	重点大学
	管得很严
	注意身体
	做这做那
	照顾自己
	比较独立
	关灯睡觉
	多吃蔬菜

II. **Listen to the recording of Dialogue 1 from Lesson 2.2 first, and then answer the True/False questions in Audio Clip 2-2-2.**

	1	2	3	4
对				
错				

III. Listen to the recording of Dialogue 2 from Lesson 2.2 first, and then answer the True/False questions in Audio Clip 2-2-3.

	1	2	3	4
对				
错				

IV. Answer the questions in this section based on your understanding of Lesson 2.2.

Directions: Listen carefully to the questions in Audio Clip 2-2-4 and record your answers on an audio recorder. If you do not have a recording device, you can write down your answers below in pinyin or characters.

1. _____

_____

_____

2. _____

_____

_____

_____

3. _____

_____

_____

4. _____

_____

_____

5. _____

_____

_____

_____

V. Each statement in Audio Clip 2-2-5 contains a conditional clause. Listen to each statement carefully for comprehension. Then read the corresponding sentence below and decide whether or not it happened. You can take notes while listening.

Model: (You will hear) 要不是我父母非要我周末回家，我一定会跟你们去海边野餐。

(You will read) 我周末跟朋友去海边野餐了。　　　T　　F

The correct answer is False.

You will hear (You can write notes here)	Statements (Did this happen?)	T/F
1.	我把家搬完了。	
2.	周末我们去南京了。	
3.	我没有参加晚会。	
4.	我不能跟你看电影。	
5.	我选了美术课。	
6.	我没有做完功课。	
7.	我们坐船去长江旅游了。	
8.	我们没有看到冰雕。	
9.	我现在很独立。	
10.	他上中学的时候谈恋爱了。	

VI. Each statement in Audio Clip 2-2-6 describes an idiom that you learned previously. First, refresh your memory by reviewing the meanings and usages of the idioms in the word bank below. Afterwards, listen to each description carefully and write down the idiom it refers to in the space provided. You can take notes while listening.

Model:

You will hear:	You will write:
这个成语的意思是，希望自己的女儿很成功。	望女成凤

Word Bank

望子成龙	掌上明珠	一心一意	一见钟情
言行一致	熟能生巧	一语中的	独生子女

Definition/Description Notes	Idiom:

二 · 综合语言练习

I. **How do you say it in Chinese?**

1. As soon as he got home, he went online to chat with his friends.

_____

2. You can do your homework now or after dinner. In any event, you have to finish your homework tonight.

_____

_____

3. It would be great if he could be independent.

_____

4. Parents shouldn't do everything for their child.

_____

5. He is already 16. Is it possible that his parents are still afraid that he won't be able to do it, or do it well?

_____

6. In some Chinese families, the whole family serves the only child.

_____

7. The teacher is very strict. Students have to do their homework.

_____

8. If not for my parents insisting that I study computer science, I would have studied art.

_____

II. **How is the "only child" treated like an emperor?**

In Dialogue 1 from Lesson 2.2, it was mentioned that "独生子女是'小皇帝,'" because "一家人都为一个孩子服务." Find some examples from the dialogue that support this statement and list them below.

III. **True or False?**

Based on Dialogue 2 from Lesson 2.2, decide whether the following statements are true or false.

	对	错
1. 星期六林东睡觉睡得很晚，因为他在网上跟同学聊天。		
2. 林东每天一回家就上网跟同学聊天。		
3. 林东觉得跟同学有说不完的话。		
4. 要不是爸爸妈妈要他回家，林东都不想回家。		
5. 林东爸爸老是问他考试考得好不好。		
6. 爸爸希望林东考上重点大学。		
7. 妈妈很注意林东的作业。		
8. 林东在学校也睡得很晚。		

IV. **Pair Activity: Is it true that...?**

Step 1: Read the following online blog post:

各位网友：

　　我不得不把这件事情告诉大家，请大家帮助我分析一下，谁对谁错。

　　上个周末，我去"飞人鞋店"买了一双运动鞋。第二天，我就穿着这双鞋去学校。可是走着走着，就觉得左脚不太舒服。我仔细(zǐxì, carefully) 一看，这两只鞋一大一小，左边的鞋是39码，右边的鞋是40码。下课以后，我马上去鞋店换鞋。

　　我把情况告诉老板以后，他说："这双鞋你已经穿过了，不可以换了。"我说："可是我不能穿一大一小的鞋啊。再说，你还有一双一大一小的鞋卖给谁呢？"他说："你说得太对了。那双一大一小的鞋我也卖不出去了，你应该把那双也买回去。"我觉得老板有问题，怎么想得出来要我买两双鞋？我只能穿40码的鞋，买一双39码的鞋做什么？可是老板说要不是因为我买鞋的时候没看清楚，就不会有这些问题了。我跟老板说了半天，可是他不但不听我的，而且还说，他让我买两双鞋是为了我好。这样，我以后买东西，就会好好检查一下了。

　　因为我不愿意买两双鞋，老板就没有给我换，所以我买回来的那双一大一小的鞋现在还放在家里。你们说，我应该怎么办？我是不是应该打电话给电视台，去抱怨一下？

Step 2: Based on the situation described above, complete the following dialogue. Be sure to use "难道⋯吗？" in your dialogue.

Model: 你难道不知道我买了一双一大一小的鞋吗？

A: **You are the customer.** **You start**	B: **You are the shoe store owner.** **Your partner starts**
• Tell B you bought a pair of shoes that are different sizes.	• Ask A if it is true that s/he didn't take a look before buying the shoes.
• Tell B you only tried the right shoe on and didn't try the left shoe. Ask B if it is true that the store should make sure the shoes are the same size.	• Ask A if it is true that s/she should find out the left shoe is too small as soon as s/he puts it on? Why did A wear the shoes for so long? Tell A you can't sell a pair of used shoes and A needs to buy the other pair that is of different sizes.
• Ask B if it is true that s/he didn't know that size 39 is too small for you. What can you do with a pair of shoes you can't wear?	• Ask A if it is true that s/he doesn't know you are doing this for her/his good? This way, A will examine goods carefully before buying them.
• Tell B you've heard enough. Ask B again if it is true that s/he is not going to change the shoes for you. If not, you are going to complain to the TV station.	• Tell A you are not going to change the shoes. Ask A if it is true that s/he doesn't know that s/he is the problem. Tell A you are going to complain to the TV station, too.

V. Mixer Activity: What's your opinion?

You are helping your school principal conduct a survey among the students. The survey is intended to find out the reasons for some common disciplinary issues. These issues are stated in Column A.

Step 1: Complete the survey by circling, in Column B, the most likely reason for each disciplinary issue. Later you will use the reason you have chosen to answer your classmates' questions.

Column A 有些学生的情况：	Column B 他们这么做是因为：	Column C 票数
1. 上课睡觉	1) 不喜欢那门课。	
	2) 他们晚上上网时间太长，睡觉睡得太晚。	
	3) 他们学习到半夜，睡觉睡得不够。	

2. 不做作业	1) 作业太难了。	
	2) 电脑坏了。	
	3) 要去打工，没时间做作业。	
3. 不来上课	1) 要在家里休息休息。	
	2) 想跟好朋友出去玩儿一天。	
	3) 不喜欢学校。	
4. 晚上不回家	1) 玩得太高兴，忘了回家。	
	2) 跟家里人关系不好。	
	3) 太晚了，在朋友家住一夜。	
5. 上课发短信	1) 在谈恋爱。	
	2) 有重要的事要告诉朋友。	
	3) 那门课没意思。	

Step 2: Following the model below, walk around the classroom to interview at least three students about what they think is the main reason for each disciplinary issue. Keep track of the interview results by keeping a tally in Column C.

Note: When answering the interviewer's questions, you must use the expression "要不是…".

Model: 问题：为什么有些学生上课睡觉？

回答：**要不是**不喜欢那门课，他们上课一定不睡觉。

问题：为什么有些学生晚上不回家？

回答：**要不是**因为他们跟家里人关系不好，他们一定会回家。

Step 3: Report your findings in class. After all the survey results are in, write a paragraph summarizing the results.

<table>
<tr><td>
给校长的报告

</td></tr>
</table>

VI. Group Activity: Do you have an excuse for this?

Work in groups of three or four. After throwing the dice, give an excuse in answer to the question or criticism by using 反正 (for example, 反正考试不难,不准备没有关系.) If you cannot come up with an excuse, you lose a turn. The first to reach the "finish" square wins the game.

START ▶	你怎么不做作业?	你怎么跟朋友聊天聊到半夜?	你怎么不打扫你的房间? ▼
你怎么吃那么多巧克力? ▼	你怎么一个星期都不运动?	你怎么不替狗洗澡?	明天要考试了,你怎么还在玩电脑游戏? ◀
你怎么做完作业不检查一下? ▶	我让你买牛奶,你怎么忘了?	你怎么那么晚才睡觉?	上课的时候,你怎么在画画儿? ▼
FINISH	你怎么不给我打电话?	你怎么又忘了把信拿进来?	你说这个月零花钱不够花,怎么又去饭店吃饭了? ◀

VII.   Group Activity: What is your relationship with your parents like?

Step 1: Complete the following questionnaire for yourself. Make sure to provide an example for each answer.

1. 父母帮你洗衣服、买东西、做饭、打扫房间吗？	
2. 父母喜欢让你独立做自己的事情吗？	
3. 如果你晚上跟朋友们出去玩儿，父母对你放心吗？	
4. 如果你在网上跟同学聊天，父母管你吗？	
5. 如果你睡觉睡得很晚，父母会不会来告诉你要早睡觉？	
6. 父母会不会老是问你考试考得怎么样？	
7. 父母对你将来的大学有什么想法？	
8. 父母多长时间检查一次你的作业？	
你觉得父母管你管得多不多？为什么？	

Step 2: Form a small group with three other students. Interview your group members using the following questions. Take notes during each interview.

When it is your turn to be interviewed, be sure to share a few concrete examples to support your answers.

访谈问题：

1. 父母对你管得严不严？

2. 你觉得在家里有机会独立做自己的事情吗？

3. 父母对你跟朋友们出去玩儿，或在网上聊天怎么看？

4. 父母常常关心你的学习吗？

5. 如果你可以对父母应该怎么管你提一些建议，你会说什么？

问题	学生姓名：	学生姓名：	学生姓名：
1.			
2.			
3.			
4.			
5.			

Step 3: Together with your group, write a summary of your interview results. At the end of your summary, make a meaningful observation about the desirable relationship between parents and teenage children. Write the summary on a separate sheet of paper and share it with your class.

汉语课：＿＿＿＿＿＿＿＿＿＿＿＿ 　　学生姓名：＿＿＿＿＿＿＿＿＿＿＿＿

日期：　＿＿＿＿＿＿＿＿＿＿＿＿

三・写作练习

Write a short essay (at least 200 characters) to compare your relationship with your family members and with your friends, using the space below or a separate piece of paper. Here are some suggestions for your essay:

1. The similarities and differences between these two relationships
2. The desirable and undesirable aspects of spending time with family members
3. The desirable and undesirable aspects of spending time with friends
4. Use a few concrete examples to support your opinions.

2.3 大家庭和小家庭
Big Families and Small Families

一 · 听力练习

I. Match Them!

Match the phrases you hear in Audio Clip 2-3-1 with the characters in Column B. Enter the corresponding numbers in Column A.

Column A 你听到的	Column B 汉字
	那么多人啊
	人多热闹
	人多意见多
	住在一起
	家里很挤
	没有自由
	说说笑笑
	跟人竞争
	进进出出
	让我数数

II. Listen to the recording of Dialogue 1 from Lesson 2.3 first, and then answer the True/False questions in Audio Clip 2-3-2.

	1	2	3	4
对				
错				

III. **Listen to the recording of Dialogue 2 from Lesson 2.3 first, and then answer the True/False questions in Audio Clip 2-3-3.**

	1	2	3	4
对				
错				

IV. **Answer the questions in this section based on your understanding of Lesson 2.3.**

Directions: Listen carefully to the questions in Audio Clip 2-3-4 and record your answers on an audio recorder. If you do not have a recording device, you can write down your answers below in pinyin or characters.

1. _____

_____

2. _____

_____

_____

3. _____

_____

_____

4. _____

_____

_____

5. _____

_____

_____

_____

_____

 V. Audio Clip 2-3-5 includes three short listening passages. Each passage is followed by two True/False questions based on its content. After listening to each passage, decide whether each statement based on the content is true or false. Each passage will be read twice.

Passage 1

a. 中国是从2005年开始一家生一个孩子的政策的。   T   F

b. 我的父母都是独生子女。所以他们可以生两个孩子。   T   F

Passage 2

a. 我的父母希望我以后上重点大学。   T   F

b. 我现在还和父母住在一起。   T   F

Passage 3

a. 我觉得学会怎么为人处事比住在一个好的环境更重要。   T   F

b. 要是我是孟子的妈妈，我也会把家搬到好的地方。   T   F

VI. Each statement in Audio Clip 2-3-6 describes a Chinese term for an extended family member that was introduced in the "Extend Your Knowledge" section of Lesson 2.3. Listen to the descriptions carefully and write down the corresponding term in the space provided. You can take notes while listening.

Model:

You will hear	You will write
这个词的意思是妈妈的姐姐或者妹妹。	阿姨

Definition/Description Notes	Name of the Family Member:
1.	
2.	
3.	
4.	
5.	
6.	
7.	
8.	
9.	
10.	

二·综合语言练习

I. How do you say it in Chinese?

1. This is our family picture. There are more than 30 people in my extended family.

_____

2. There are two small beds in my room. My sister and I share the room.

_____

3. There are people coming and going, chatting and laughing, every day in our house. It is extremely lively.

_____

4. Having more people means having more opinions, which makes it difficult to come to a decision.

_____

5. In a large family, it is impossible to get any quiet time.

_____

6. Even though an only child does not need to compete with other children at home, he does not have other children to play with either.

_____

_____

7. Although my parents always take care of me, I feel they control me too much.

_____

8. Can it be true that you want your grandparents to control you 24 hours a day?

_____

II. Grandma Zhang's Family

Maria is fascinated by Grandma Zhang's family. After talking to Grandma Zhang (see Dialogue 1 from Lesson 2.3), she wrote an email to her friend. See if Maria has got all the facts straight.

Send	Reply	Reply All	Forward	Print	Delete

明英：你好！

　　昨天你打电话给我的时候，我正在张爷爷家呢。真是对不起，不能跟你一起去打网球。等下次吧。

　　张奶奶昨天告诉我，中国以前有许多大家庭。张奶奶也是在大家庭里长大的。他们家有十八个人。你想得出来十八个人住在一起会是什么样的吗？我们家现在才五个人，但是我觉得已经很挤了。可是张奶奶说那时候他们家十八个都住在一个很小的房子里，每个房间有两个大床，要睡五个人。张奶奶有四个姐姐，她们姐妹五个都睡在一个房间里。

　　除了张奶奶一家以外，她爷爷奶奶、大叔叔一家和小叔叔一家也住在哪儿。她两个叔叔都只有男孩子，没有女孩子。那么多人每天在一起吃饭。张奶奶说，那时候他们家分三个桌子吃饭，大人一桌，男孩子一桌，女孩子一桌。每天张奶奶的奶奶做饭就要做七八个小时。

　　大家庭的生活很神奇 (shénqí, amazing) 吧？

玛丽娅

If you have found any discrepancies between what Grandma Zhang said and what Maria wrote, list them in the following table:

张奶奶说的和玛丽娅写的，有这些不同：

III. The Positive and Negative Aspects of Being an Only Child

Based on Dialogue 2 from Lesson 2.3, decide whether the following statements about being an only child are true or false.

	对	不对
1) 在家没有人跟独生子女竞争玩具。		
2) 在家没有人跟独生子女竞争吃的东西。		
3) 独生子女要什么，父母总是会给什么。		
4) 什么电视节目，独生子女都可以看。		
5) 在家里，独生子女常常跟大人玩。		
6) 有时候，独生子女也可以去公园跟小朋友玩。		
7) 父母常常二十四小时都管着独生子女。		
8) 独生子女可以拿到很多零花钱。		
9) 因为被很多人管，独生子女没有很多的自由。		
10) 独生子女被家里很多人关心照顾。		

IV. Pair Activity: Everything Has Two Sides

You and your partner are going to compare the advantages and disadvantages of having a large or small family.

Step 1: Work as individuals to think of three sentences that describe the advantages and disadvantages of having a small or a large family. Write down your sentences in the space below. Be sure to use 虽然···可是··· in your sentences.

Model: 小家庭虽然不热闹，但是做决定比较快。

　　　　　大家庭虽然热闹，但是做决定比较慢。

A's worksheet: You write about a small family.

1.	
2.	
3.	

B's worksheet: You write about a large family.

1.	
2.	
3.	

Step 2: Share your sentences with your partner. Work together to fill out the following summary chart:

	长处	短处
小家庭	1. 做决定快 2. 3. 4. 5.	1. 不热闹 2. 3. 4. 5.
大家庭	1. 热闹 2. 3. 4. 5.	1. 做决定慢 2. 3. 4. 5.

Step 3: Share your summary in class. Make sure that your discussion is in Chinese only.

V. Online Chat Room

You are in an online chat room. A Chinese high school student is interested in learning about American families because next semester he will be coming to America as an exchange student. As part of the exchange program, he is going to live with an American family. Try to help him by giving him some information and advice.

网友一： 在美国大家庭多还是小家庭多？

网友二： 很难说。有的家庭有两三个孩子，有的有五六个。

网友一： 有那么多孩子啊？你们家也有那么多孩子吗？

你： _____

网友三： 我们家有三个孩子。

网友一： 美国独生子女多不多？

你： _____

网友一： 你们跟爷爷奶奶或者姥姥姥爷住在一起吗？

你： _____

网友一： 那如果爷爷奶奶年龄大了，谁照顾他们呢？

网友二： 我爷爷奶奶都住在老人院。老人院里的人照顾他们。

你： 我爷爷奶奶_____

网友一： 一般的美国家庭是不是住在很大的房子里？

你： _____

网友一： 你们跟父母住在一个房间里吗？

网友二： 在美国，孩子常常有自己的房间。在中国呢？

网友一： 要看。有的人家房子比较大，孩子有自己的房间。房子小
的话，一家人可能就住在一个房间里。我家只有一个房间
和一个客厅，所以我睡在客厅里。你们呢？

你： _____

网友三： 我家有三个房间，父母一间，我和我弟弟一间，我姐姐一
间。

网友一： 是不是每个美国家庭都有电脑？可以上网？

你： _____

网友一： 如果在家不能上网，你们去哪儿上网？

你： _____

网友一： 谢谢你，告诉我这么多关于美国的事。

VI. **Pair Activity: Tell me about one of your relatives!**

Pair up with a partner and ask her/him questions to find out as much detail as you can about one of her/his relatives. You can use the conversation card below as a guide when asking questions. Record your partner's answers in the space provided.

Conversation Card

1. Find out how many siblings your partner's parents have.
2. Decide to ask follow-up questions about one of the siblings or relatives.
3. Ask about this relative's biographical information (name, age, residence, profession, etc.).
4. Ask whether this relative is married or has children.
5. Ask your partner to share one unique thing about this relative.
6. **Switch! It's your partner's turn to ask about your relatives.**

我朋友的亲戚

VII. **Oral Presentation: Meet my extended family!**

Draw a family tree showing your extended family and give a presentation about the maternal or paternal relatives. Your presentation must include as many details as possible. Be sure to use a variety of vocabulary and expressions.

汉语课：_____   学生姓名：_____

日期：_____

三·写作练习

Choose one advantage or disadvantage of having a small or a large family from the summary chart in Part Two: Integrated Language Practice, Activity IV. This will be the theme of a three-paragraph essay. In your essay, you need to use two or more examples to support your opinion and include a few details for each example. Your essay should contain at least 200 characters and must include the following sections on the space below or a separate piece of paper:

1. Introduction paragraph: Clearly state your thesis statement. For example, 我觉得大家庭比较好，因为··· (give a reason).
2. Body - second paragraph: Give two or more examples that support your statement.
3. Conclusion - third paragraph: You can acknowledge that there are always two sides to a situation (虽然···但是···). But after weighing the pros and cons, you still feel a large (or small) family is better.

_____

_____

_____

_____

_____

_____

_____

_____

跨国家庭
A Multinational Family

一・听力练习

I. Match Them!

Match the phrases you hear in Audio Clip 2-4-1 with the phrases you read in Column B. Enter the corresponding numbers in Column A.

Column A 你听到的	Column B 汉字
	电视节目
	经济发展
	越来越多
	家庭生活
	跨国家庭
	祖祖辈辈
	马马虎虎
	各国移民
	各国文化
	各国甜点

II. Listen to the recording of Dialogue 1 from Lesson 2.4 first, and then answer the True/False questions in Audio Clip 2-4-2.

	1	2	3	4
对				
错				

III. Listen to the recording of Dialogue 2 from Lesson 2.4 first, and then answer the True/False questions in Audio Clip 2-4-3.

	1	2	3	4
对				
错				

IV. Answer the questions in this section based on your understanding of Lesson 2.4.

Directions: Listen carefully to the questions in Audio Clip 2-4-4 and record your answers on an audio recorder. If you do not have a recording device, you can write down your answers below in pinyin or characters.

1. _____

_____

2. _____

_____

_____

_____

3. _____

_____

_____

_____

4. _____

_____

_____

5. _____

_____

_____

_____

6. _____

_____

_____

V. Rejoinders: In Audio Clip 2-4-5 you will hear five partial conversations, followed by four possible choices designated (A), (B), (C), and (D). Circle the choice that continues or completes the conversation in a logical and culturally appropriate manner.

Note: Both the questions and the choices will be read only once.

1	2	3	4	5
(A)	(A)	(A)	(A)	(A)
(B)	(B)	(B)	(B)	(B)
(C)	(C)	(C)	(C)	(C)
(D)	(D)	(D)	(D)	(D)

VI. Each statement in Audio Clip 2-4-6 describes a proverb that you earned in your second year of study. First, refresh your memory and review the meanings and usages of the proverbs in the word bank below. Afterwards listen to each description carefully and write down the proverb it refers to in the space provided. You may take notes while listening.

Model:

You will hear:	You will write:
这个成语的意思是，希望自己的女儿很成功。	望女成凤

Word Bank

车水马龙	学富五车	一路平安	多多益善
好好先生	说一不二	老马识途	山南海北

Definition/Description Notes	Proverbs:
1.	
2.	
3.	
4.	
5.	
6.	
7.	
8.	

二·综合语言练习

I. How do you say it in Chinese?

1. Now there are more and more multinational families.

_____

2. More and more families are like small United Nations.

_____

3. In the past the Chinese lived in one place for generations.

_____

4. Now the economy has developed and many people have moved to other places to work.

_____

5. I am very lucky to be able to celebrate the festivals of many countries.

_____

6. Although he has a slight Chinese accent, he speaks French very well.

_____

7. When Teacher Zhang is anxious, he speaks faster and faster.

_____

8. Because my grandparents are from Shanghai, they feel everything from Shanghai is good.

_____

II. Multinational Families

Based on Dialogue 1 from Lesson 2.4, decide whether the following statements are true or false:

	对	错
1. "跨国家庭"就是说，家里的人不是从一个国家来的。		
2. 跨国家庭在一些国家不算新鲜事。		
3. 在移民比较多的国家，跨国家庭比较多。		
4. 虽然中国移民不多，但是跨国家庭也非常多。		
5. 以前中国人祖祖辈辈住在一个地方。		
6. 现在因为经济发展了，差不多每个中国人都离开家去别的地方工作。		
7. 有不少外国人到中国来工作，但是中国人一般不愿意去外国。		
8. 现在中国人和外国人结婚的越来越多，跨国家庭也越来越多了。		

III. Kelly's Family

Based on Dialogues 1 and 2 from Lesson 2.4, fill out the following chart with the details you can discover about Kelly's and Tom's grandparents.

凯丽	爷爷	
	奶奶	
	姥爷	
	姥姥	
汤姆	爷爷	
	奶奶	
	姥爷	
	姥姥	

IV. Group Activity: What does that word mean?

Step 1: Form a group of four students. Select one person as the game show host and the other three as contestants.

Step 2: The host will ask the contestants to give a definition to a term randomly selected from the list below. If the contestant doesn't know the answer, s/he can pass the turn to the next contestant. Each correct answer is worth10 points. Each incorrect answer or unanswered question subtracts 10 points.

Model: 问题："新鲜事"是什么意思?

回答：是以前没有听说过或者看到过的事。

马马虎虎	移民	邻居	结婚
跨国家庭	祖祖辈辈	外国人	同意
全家福	越来越多	亲戚	国外

Step 3: The host tallies the points to find out who the winner is.

	Contestant 1	Contestant 2	Contestant 3
总分 (total points)			

V. Pair Activity: The Current Situation in Our School

Step 1: Work on your own. Fill out the following questionnaire about your school. You should list at least three situations in each column.

你觉得这一年里学校有什么变化？哪些情况越来越好？哪些情况越来越不好？校长需要了解学生们的意见，这样可以更好地为学生服务。(The first item is an example. You don't have to include it on your list).

越来越好	越来越不好
同学们越来越注意健康。	教室楼越来越旧。
1.	1.
2.	2.
3.	3.
4.	4.
5.	5.

Step 2: Take turns to tell your partner what you feel about your school. Listen to your partner carefully to see if s/he agrees with you on any issues.

Step 3: Report the issues that you and your partner agree on to the class. Use "越来越."

Model: 我们都觉得，同学们越来越注意健康。

VI. Group Activity: International Dinner Menu Competition

Step 1: Form a small group of three or four students. Each student in the group selects a country and creates a list of foods to be included on the menu. The list must include at least one appetizer, one soup or salad, one main entrée, and one dessert.

_____国食品	
头台	
色拉/汤	
主菜	
甜点	

Step 2: Share your list with your group. Together with your group, design a menu. Your menu must be decorated to reflect its multicultural nature.

Step 3: Share your menu with your class. Select one person from your group to introduce your menu to the class. Your introduction must include the following information:

1. Which countries/cultures gave your group inspiration in creating this menu?
2. What dishes does your menu offer (you may want to present the dishes by category)?
3. Why have you decided to offer these dishes (family recipe, etc.)?

Step 4: Vote for the best menu and ask your teacher if the class could host an international food day!

VII. Group Activity: My Multicultural Family

Task: To understand the multicultural aspects of our families.

Step 1: Interview your parents or grandparents and find out your family's roots. For example, find out where your family members originally came from (this can be a country or a region), when they moved to their current location, and how they feel about the culture/region/country that they were originally from. Enter your interview results in the table below.

问题	爸爸家	妈妈家
最早是从哪儿来的？		
哪年搬到这里来的？		
为什么搬到这里来的？		
搬来以后有没有不适应的地方？		
觉得这里的文化跟以前住的地方有什么不同？		
喜欢或不喜欢这里文化的什么地方？		
跟原来的文化还有什么联系？		

Step 2: Form a small group of four students. Share your family's roots with your group. While listening, fill out the following information cards for each family:

学生姓名：	爸爸家	妈妈家
最早是从哪儿来的？		
哪年搬到这里来的？		
为什么搬到这里来的？		
搬来以后有没有不适应的地方？		
觉得这里的文化跟以前住的地方有什么不同？		
喜欢或不喜欢这里文化的什么地方？		
跟原来的文化还有什么联系？		

学生姓名：	爸爸家	妈妈家
最早是从哪儿来的？		
哪年搬到这里来的？		
为什么搬到这里来的？		
搬来以后有没有不适应的地方？		
觉得这里的文化跟以前住的地方有什么不同？		
喜欢或不喜欢这里文化的什么地方？		
跟原来的文化还有什么联系？		

学生姓名：	爸爸家	妈妈家
最早是从哪儿来的？		
哪年搬到这里来的？		
为什么搬到这里来的？		
搬来以后有没有不适应的地方？		
觉得这里的文化跟以前住的地方有什么不同？		
喜欢或不喜欢这里文化的什么地方？		
跟原来的文化还有什么联系？		

汉语课：＿＿＿＿＿＿＿＿＿　　　学生姓名：＿＿＿＿＿＿＿＿

日期：　＿＿＿＿＿＿＿＿＿

三·写作练习

A local non-profit organization has sought your help in preparing a Chinese-language brochure for newcomers to your city or town. In addition to the essential information on utility companies, schools, medical facilities, and so on, the non-profit organization would like to include short descriptions of some "featured places" to reflect the cultural diversity of your city/town. You are asked to contribute a short description (no more than 100 characters) to the brochure.

The following list is for your reference.

博物馆	学校	旅游点	特别的商店
饭店	体育运动	文化节日	娱乐活动

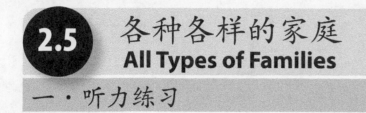

各种各样的家庭
All Types of Families

一・听力练习

I. Match Them!

Match the phrases you hear in Audio Clip 2-5-1 with the Chinese characters in Column B. Enter the corresponding numbers in Column A.

Column A 你听到的	Column B 意思
	同父异母
	同母异父
	互相照顾
	互相关心
	父母离婚
	父母再婚
	同父同母
	单亲家庭
	建立家庭
	各种各样

II. Listen to the recording of the Lesson 2.5 Dialogue first, and then answer the True/False questions in Audio Clip 2-5-2.

	1	2	3	4
对				
错				

III. Listen to the recording of the Lesson 2.5 Text first, and then answer the True/False questions in Audio Clip 2-5-3.

	1	2	3	4
对				
错				

IV. Answer the questions in this section based on your understanding of Lesson 2.5.

Directions: Listen carefully to the questions in Audio Clip 2-5-4 and record your answers on an audio recorder. If you do not have a recording device, you can write down your answers below in pinyin or characters.

1. _____

_____

_____

2. _____

_____

_____

_____

3. _____

_____

_____

_____

_____

_____

4. _____

_____

_____

_____

_____

_____

5. _____

_____

_____

_____

_____

_____

_____

_____

_____

_____

6. _____

V. Audio Clip 2-5-5 includes three short listening passages. Each passage is followed by two true or false questions based on the content. After listening to each passage, decide whether each statement based on the content is true or false. Each passage will be read twice.

<u>Passage 1</u>

  a. 中国的孩子们觉得很难记住怎么叫家里的亲戚。   T   F

  b. 中国的父母也不太清楚家里的亲戚怎么叫。   T   F

<u>Passage 2</u>

  a. 要是一个中国家庭只能送一个孩子上学，那他们
     常常把不太聪明的孩子送到学校，因为聪明的
     孩子可以自己学习。   T   F

  b. 孩子从学校毕业以后，要照顾家里的人。   T   F

<u>Passage 3</u>

  a. 中国人觉得结婚、生孩子很重要。因为有了孩子以后，
     孩子们以后会照顾你。   T   F

  b. 在中国，要是你二十几岁没有男朋友或者女朋友，
     你父母会帮助你找一个。   T   F

VI. Each statement in Audio Clip 2-5-6 describes an idiom that you learned in your second year of study. First, refresh your memory by reviewing the meanings and usages of the idioms in the word bank below. Afterwards listen to each description carefully and write down the idiom it refers to in the space provided. You can take notes while listening.

Model:

You will hear	You will write
这个成语的意思是，希望自己的女儿很成功。	望女成凤

Word Bank

一鸣惊人	五湖四海	一五一十	花好月圆
水中捞月	如鱼得水	鸡毛蒜皮	人山人海

Definition/Description Notes	Idiom

二·综合语言练习

I. How do you say it in Chinese?

1. Five years ago, her parents divorced. Later her mother remarried.

_____

2. Now she has a younger stepbrother (same mother, different fathers).

_____

3. Her stepfather has two other children, but they don't live with him.

_____

4. Her father hasn't remarried and doesn't plan to get remarried.

_____

5. A traditional Chinese family has three generations living together.

_____

6. In the last several decades, Chinese families have had great changes.

_____

7. Some young people like freedom, so they move out of their parents' home and live by themselves.

_____

8. Family members should be concerned about each other, help each other, and take care of each other.

_____

II. Jin Shun'ai's Family

Fill in the missing information in the paragraph below based on the Lesson 2.5 Dialogue. The words that you may use are given in the word bank.

Word Bank:

同父异母	同父同母	同母异父	继父	继母
离婚	再婚	妈妈	跨国家庭	

金顺爱的家庭

　　金顺爱的家庭是一个_____。她家有五口人。继父、妈妈、两个弟弟和她。她八岁的时候，父母_____了。她和她弟弟都跟她_____生活。金顺爱的妈妈后来再婚了。_____是一个中国人。她妈妈和继父都是律师，现在在上海工作。她的两个弟弟，一个跟她_____，一个跟她_____。

　　金顺爱的爸爸还住在韩国。他也_____了。现在家里有四口人。金顺爱的_____很年轻，才二十六岁。金顺爱有两个_____的小妹妹。一个四岁，一个两岁。

III. Chinese Families, Past and Present

List the different types of family mentioned in the Lesson 2.5 Text and explain the typical characteristics of these families.

不同的中国家庭：

IV. Pair Activity: By the way...

You and your partner are comparing information that you've received about an upcoming school-organized field trip.

Both of you got your information from a disorganized teacher, Teacher Wang. Take turns telling your partner what you heard from Teacher Wang. While your partner speaks, listen carefully. If your partner has missed some information, you need to give him or her additional information.

Model: **A:** 王老师说，我们七点从学校出发。

B: 对了，王老师还说，客车要七点十分左右才能来。

A's sheet

你开始	星期六早上七点从学校出发。
你同学开始	去的人太多，另外还有一辆小客车。
你开始	路上要三个小时。
你同学开始	先去参观博物馆，然后去吃午饭。
你开始	吃完午饭是自由活动。
你同学开始	五点半才离开那里回学校。

B's sheet

你同学开始	客车要七点十分左右才能来。
你开始	一共有两辆大客车。
你同学开始	现在可以走新的公路，两个半小时可以到了。
你开始	到了以后先去吃午饭。
你同学开始	除了自由活动以外，他还要带我们去坐游船。
你开始	四点半就要离开那里回学校。

V. **Mixer Bingo: Great Minds Think Alike**

Step 1: Read through the following living situations and circle nine that you think are pretty good. Write these situations in your bingo grid.

1. 跟父母住在一起
2. 跟父母，爷爷奶奶住在一起
3. 跟父亲和继母住在一起
4. 跟母亲和继父住在一起
5. 跟爷爷奶奶住在一起
6. 不跟兄弟姐妹住在一起
7. 跟兄弟姐妹住在一起
8. 跟同父异母的兄弟姐妹住在一起
9. 跟同母异父的兄弟姐妹住在一起
10. 你一个人
11. 跟好朋友住在一起
12. 住在朋友的家
13. 已经结婚了，有自己的小家庭
14. 跟许多亲戚住在一个大家庭里
15. 跟男朋友住在一起
16. 跟女朋友住在一起

Step 2: Circulate around the classroom and ask your classmates if they think a particular living situation is good. You can only ask each student one question. When a student answers "Yes" to a question, cross the square out. You win the game if you successfully cross out three questions in a row.

Model: 问题：你喜欢住在朋友家吗？

回答：喜欢。(Or 不喜欢。)

Bingo Card

VI. You've got mail!

Your friend, Mark, has graduated from high school and is thinking about his living situation. He sent you the following email. Read the email and write a 50-character summary of the email content.

Send	Reply	Reply All	Forward	Print	Delete

几个月没见了，你好吗？这几个月，我挺忙的。高中毕业以后，我就开始在超市工作。因为我是新去的，经理安排我上夜班。每天晚上10点去上班，到第二天早上7点下班。我的工作是把第二天超市里要卖的食品准备好。同事都挺好的，工作还不错。

不过，这两个星期，有一件事让我挺头疼的。我妈妈决定要跟她的男朋友结婚。她男朋友叫科文，对我妈妈和我都挺好的。我为妈妈高兴，她又要有一个新家庭了。我妈妈说，她结婚以后，我可以跟她一起搬到科文家去住。可是科文有两个儿子。我觉得我跟他们住在一起会不舒服。妈妈说，要是我不愿意跟她住，可以去我爸爸那里。

　　我爸爸的房子很大，有地方让我住。他也再婚了，我有两个同父异母的妹妹，她们很可爱，也对我很好。可是我不太喜欢我的继母，她话多得不得了，从早到晚都在说一些没有用的话。再说，我爸爸挺怕她的。她说什么我爸爸都说"对，对，对，好，好，好。"

　　想来想去，我打算自己住。可是一个人住比较贵，因为我刚工作，又买了一辆新车，所以还没有很多钱。你有什么建议吗？

马克

Summary:

_____

_____

_____

_____

汉语课: _____   学生姓名: _____
日期: _____

三・写作练习

Write a response with approximately 150 Chinese characters to Mark's email (see Activity VI above). Tell him what you think he should do.

Send	Reply	Reply All	Forward	Print	Delete

第二单元复习
Review of Unit 2

一·口头报告

Choose one of the topics from the list below to give an oral presentation in class. Your presentation must meet the following criteria:

(1) It must have a beginning, a middle, and an end.
(2) It must include as much detail as possible.
(3) It must last no more than two minutes.

After you have chosen the topic, please write an outline for your presentation. You can write the outline on a separate sheet of paper. If your teacher allows, you can also transfer the outline to an index card as a reminder when you give the presentation.

Topic 1. 梁山伯和祝英台：中国的爱情故事

Topic 2. 孟母三迁：父母对孩子的爱

Topic 3. 照顾老人是我们的责任

Topic 4. 什么样的家庭是快乐家庭？

Topic 5. 中学生应该谈恋爱吗？

Topic 6. 独生子女的快乐

Topic 7. 我爱我的大家庭

Topic 8. 我跟父母的关系

二·综合语言练习

I. Did Maria get all the facts right?

玛丽娅对丁老师说：

　　丁老师，你说过以前中国人祖祖辈辈住在一个地方。因为最近经济发展很快，城市里的工作多了，许多住在农村的人都到城里来找工作。有些人还搬家到城里来。那天，我跟汤姆聊天，他告诉我他有一个农村的亲戚，在北京找到了工作，一家人就搬到北京去住了。可是因为住在北京很贵，所以他家的人又搬回到农村去住，现在只有他一个人还住在北京。汤姆的亲戚只有过年过节的时候才能回家，一年只能回去两三次。这个亲戚的父母妻子和孩子都在农村，他们都很喜欢农村的生活，不喜欢住在城市里。结果汤姆的亲戚现在打算要回农村去，到那里去开个小公司，这样他就可以跟家里人住在一起了。

Based on Dialogue 1 from Lesson 2.6, list at least three correct and three incorrect facts that Maria talked about.

玛丽娅说得对	玛丽娅说得不对

II. A Big Family

Based on Dialogue 2 from Lesson 2.6, list all the people and animals in Uncle Zhang's household. Add a short note to explain why they are there (if the reason is mentioned in the dialogue).

家庭成员 (family member)	为什么住在张叔叔家？
张叔叔	男主人

III. The Most Diverse Family Contest

To celebrate cultural diversity, the local Chinese immigrant community is sponsoring an online "Multinational Family of the Year" contest. People can enter the contest by sending in a short description of their family with no more than 50 Chinese characters. The site encourages everyone to vote for the "Multinational Family of the Year."

Step 1: Cast your vote

为为	爷爷奶奶来自中国，姥爷姥姥来自韩国，可是姥姥的父母也来自中国。我是不是75%中国人，25%韩国人呢？	☺☺☺☺☺
小马	爸爸是中国人，继母也是中国人。妈妈是美国人，继父是中日混 (hùn, mixed) 血 (xuè, blood)。	☺☺☺☺☺
老张	我大儿子跟意大利人、小儿子跟南非人、大女儿跟德国人、小女儿跟美国人结婚了。	☺☺☺☺☺
丁丁	我是半个中国人半个德国人。同父异母的弟弟是半个中国人半个法国人，同母异父的妹妹是半个德国人半个加拿大人。	☺☺☺☺☺
冰冰	不知道我父母是哪国人。我现在的爸爸是美国人。爷爷在英国出生，奶奶是在中国出生的美国人。	☺☺☺☺☺
美英	我是北京人，先生是美国人，他有三个小孩，三个小孩的妈妈是：英国人、澳大利亚人和马里人。	☺☺☺☺☺

Step 2: Compare your answers with three students and see whether you've reached the same conclusion.

IV. Class Debate: Everything Has Two Sides

Divide the class into two teams.

Step 1: Work as a team. Use the topics below to prepare for a debate. Try to come up with as many explanations as possible to support your team's position.

Team A

A队的意见	因为
1. 大家庭比较好	
2. 做独生子女比较好	
3. 早一点儿谈恋爱好	

Team B

B队的意见	因为
1. 小家庭比较好	
2. 兄弟姐妹多比较好	
3. 晚一点儿谈恋爱好	

Step 2: Hold the debate. Your teacher will be the judge.

V. Group Activity: He said..., she said...

Form a group of four.

Step 1: Work in pairs. Interview your partner to learn about his or her family.

Step 2: Switch partners. Tell your second partner what you have learned about your first partner's family.

Step 3: Switch partners again. The second partner will tell the first partner what s/he has heard from you. The first partner can check if both of you have got it right.

VI. Can you construct a logical story?

After Mark finished his homework on the computer, he forgot to save it before taking a break. When he came back from the break, he saw his toddler brother playing with the mouse. Somehow the little guy moved around some sentences in the article. See if you can help Mark to reconstruct the story by putting the sentences in the correct order.

___我父亲和母亲是在纽约上大学的时候认识的。他们大学还没有毕业就结婚了。

___结婚后过了一年，我就出生了。

___我出生以后，妈妈就退学了，在家照顾我。

___我爸爸大学毕业以后当了律师，他总是很忙，每天很晚回家，跟我妈妈越来越没有话说。

___有一天，我妈妈决定要把我送到姥姥家去，让姥姥照顾我，她自己要回大学去把课修完。

___我爸爸听了我妈妈的决定以后，非常不高兴，觉得她没有把家庭放在第一。

___可是我妈妈说，我爸爸没有想到她。因为这件事，他们的关系越来越不好。

___我妈妈从大学毕业以后，他们就离婚了。

___我十三岁的时候，我妈妈再婚了。我继父是一位作家，他很爱我妈妈，对我也很好。前两年，我又有了一个小弟弟。他非常可爱，看到我做什么，就要做什么。

___对了，我爸爸现在一个人住，他跟我妈妈离婚以后，又结过两次婚，可是又都离婚了。所以，我还有两个同父异母的妹妹。

CREDITS

Murray Thomas contributed the following drawings:

4, 15, 47, 51, 66, 75, 76, 77, 85, 86, 89, 123, 138

Landong Xu contributed the following drawings:

5, 7, 20, 29, 52, 72, 73, 111, 123, 146

Augustine Liu contributed the following drawings:

9